Patrick Whitworth, author of *Becoming Fully Human, Becoming a Spiritual Leader* and *Becoming a Citizen of the Kingdom* is Rector of All Saints, Weston, and Rural Dean of Bath. He was Curate of Holy Trinity Brompton following a first curacy at St Michael-le-Belfrey, York, where he served under David Watson. He is Canon of Bauchi Diocese in Nigeria and is Chairman of the UK SOMA Council. He is married to Olivia and they have four children.

D1076911

To my parents,
who inspired me to grasp the past
in order to peer into the future

PREPARE FOR EXILE

A new spirituality and mission
for the church

Martyn –

[I]TWORTH

Thought I'd send
you another book
written by our Rector.
I don't know how he
finds time to write
so much while running
three churches!.

I found this an
interesting read –
            love from

                Ros –

Best In
Show

Ⓚ

First published in Great Britain in 2008

Society for Promoting Christian Knowledge
36 Causton Street
London SW1P 4ST

British Library Cataloguing-in-Publication Data
A catalogue record for this book is available from the British Library

ISBN 978–0–281–06003–0

1 3 5 7 9 10 8 6 4 2

Typeset by Graphicraft Ltd, Hong Kong
Printed in Great Britain by Ashford Colour Press

Produced on paper from sustainable forests

Contents

Contents

Foreword

Exile is a theme that runs right through the Bible. If some commentators are to be believed it is the dominant theme, with much of the Old Testament written or re-edited in the light of the traumatic experience of Israel's exile in Babylon and Assyria, and the ministry of Jesus dominated by the yearning for the end of exile – the subjection of the nation to foreign powers. It remains a haunting and resonant theme in contemporary life, with refugees roaming the world from Palestine to Darfur to Somalia and countless other places.

In this book, Patrick Whitworth explores the theme of exile as a metaphor for the condition of the church in the UK. Used to centuries of prominence at the centre of culture, it increasingly finds itself pushed to the edges, banished from the corridors of power and decision-making. Yet, as he wisely points out, times of exile have often been the most creative in the history of Israel and the church. Exile makes people re-evaluate what is important, adapt to new conditions and rediscover their true identity, which can often get blurred during periods of prosperity and ease. And that is the exciting opportunity the church has at this precise moment.

Patrick ranges over an impressive range of material here – from biblical studies to the history of the church to contemporary culture, to analyse this theme. He suggests that in this time of unsettling exile, the church needs to develop new patterns of mission, spirituality and community to adapt and thrive in a new world. This is no easy path – it is costly, yet promises much. As he puts it, 'exile has often been the price of change, renewal and, at times, revival.'

In exile, people can either assimilate so that they lose their identity, withdraw into themselves and slowly die off, or adapt creatively while retaining a vital sense of what makes them different. That is the challenge for today's church, a challenge laid down by this book. It explores an evocative and rich theme for understanding the place of the church in contemporary British life. It is well worth reading, studying and debating, and has an important message which I hope will be heard widely.

Graham Tomlin

Preface

Today as I write this Preface there is a two-page spread in *The Times* written by their chief religious correspondent, Ruth Gledhill, based upon the publication *Religious Trends*, and with the arresting headline, 'Churchgoing on its knees as Christianity falls out of favour' (8 May 2008). And conveniently (for the purposes of the article) an empty church in Hampstead is taken as the accompanying photograph. The church attendance figures extrapolated from present rates of decline or growth (in some parts of the church) across the denominations show that in 2050 the churchgoing population in Britain will be only 899,000, the same as the number of Hindus and less than the number of Muslims. Whatever the truth behind 'damn lies and statistics', and whatever the actual situation in 2050 (I probably won't be here to see it), the article goes on to say that such a loss of God as revealed by Christ will leave a sense of loss of national identity. We could face a culture of secularism and consumerism in a mixture of religious affiliations in which government arbitrates between competing religious claims on its attention, purse strings and legislative power.

But the church and God's people, at least in the biblical narrative and in the early years of its life, is no stranger to exile. Perhaps we are returning to such a situation again. If so, we need to admit as much, prepare ourselves for it, seek God's renewal in it, and draw strength and inspiration from our foundation documents, which talk about exile in the past, as well as remembering the exiles in church history. If we have reached a new historical paradigm, which is now especially dominant in northern Europe, and which feels it has outgrown Christianity and knows better, how are we to sing the Lord's song in a foreign land? That is the question posed, if not answered (for who has all the answers?) in this book.

My hope is that it will make us pray, hope, talk, perceive what is going on, review our attitudes, spirituality and mission in the light of exile, and perhaps above all return to the exilic prophets for some answers, remembering that when the people of God were in exile their hope was renewed, a new covenant was promised and new examples of courage were provided.

Preface

My thanks to all those who helped in this book's production; to SPCK for their willingness to take it on and their help with the refining process; to Gay Carder and Ann Banner for their help with the bibliography and the 'production process'; and to my family for putting up with those hours of 'exile' in a little room in our Church Centre. It almost goes without saying that all the shortcomings in fact, perception or conclusions are entirely mine.

Patrick Whitworth,
8 May 2008, the feast day of Mother Julian of Norwich
(another exile or anchoress, this time in a small
room in a church in Norwich)

Introduction

The question we are considering in this book is whether the church today in Britain, and to a certain extent in Northern Europe, is facing a kind of exile. And if it is, what kind of an exile is it? What can be learnt usefully from the experience of exile as recorded in the Bible as well as from the wealth of experience from individuals and groups who have experienced exile in their own day? And again, if we, as the Christian community, are facing a kind of exile presently in Britain, then what effect does this have upon our mission, our spirituality and our attitudes? These are some of the important questions we will consider in this book.

In part this book is about the place that exile has played and still plays in the history and development of the Jewish and then the Christian faith. The story cannot be comprehensive because there is too much material to deal with in such a short book, but by touching on it we can see that the theme and indeed the reality of exile is important to Jewish faith-history as well as to Christian self-understanding. Indeed, much of the Old Testament is about anticipating, warning and then experiencing the reality of exile as both a punitive and a refining experience in the life of the Jewish nation. It is not an exaggeration to say that about a third of the Old Testament is taken up with dealing, in one way or another, with the theme of exile: there is the warning by the Prophets of its coming, the record of its actual happening, and then the making sense of its significance and finally putting into practice its lessons. And since the Roman destruction of Jerusalem in AD 70 and its rebuilding as Aelia Capitolina by Hadrian in AD 135, the story of the Jewish people is for the most part a story of a nation in almost permanent exile until the resettlement of Palestine by the Jews after the First World War.

Christianity too, especially in its early years as we shall see, experienced a real sense of exile. But from Constantine's settlement of the early fourth century, tying the church to the state in a construction which came to be called Christendom and which existed until the latter part of the twentieth century, church and state in Europe became more or less synonymous or coterminous with each other.

We shall trace this later in the book. This period of Christendom particularly in Europe lasted for around seventeen hundred years and its legacy is still to be seen.

Yet often in these years there were both individuals and movements which themselves experienced exile. They expressed the Christian faith in ways that challenged the accepted or state-backed formulations of Christianity. These movements of exile, as I shall call them, resisted what they saw as false teaching or corruption. They insisted on reforming or renewing the church and challenged leaders with criticism they were usually unwilling to face. On account of these challenges they were often sent into exile themselves and many suffered the final exile, death itself, which was seen by them as the ultimate homecoming.

There are some countries which specialize in sending people into exile, none more so than Russia. Whether ruled by the Tsars, the Communist authorities or by the more centralizing tendencies of the present Russian government, exile was and is a ready tool of political and religious repression. Perhaps this should not be all that surprising, since the country comprises such huge areas of arctic tundra to which the unwanted can be easily banished. Siberia and its wastelands can swallow up any number of exiles into a kind of frozen anonymity where they can be forgotten or, if remembered, their memory is a salutary warning to others. But others in church history, not least among them the Desert Fathers and Mothers, chose a self-imposed exile: a kind of denial of the world in order to pray for the church and society. They included people like St Anthony, made famous by Athanasius, and Simeon Stylites, who in the fifth century sat on a pillar or rock outside Aleppo giving spiritual advice to all comers. So exile came in all kinds of ways and to some countries more easily than others.

But there have been times when church and government were not synonymous, and the church faced a kind of collective exile. In European history this occurred, for instance, in France briefly during and after the French Revolution when pagan classical symbols were attached to parish churches, the Christian calendar, Christian symbols and clerical leadership were suppressed. But more especially it occurred in Communist Eastern Europe where the church was either actively persecuted or permitted to exist only if it agreed to support the state, leading to a debate about whether or not Christians were right to work with the state and thus avoid persecution. We live now in a period of history when the Communist suppression of Christianity in Eastern Europe is still in the recent past and the role of the church is still being evaluated. However, the question for us to consider is whether the church in Britain faces a new kind of exile in the pluralist and secular culture which has come to dominate Northern Europe especially, and if so what difference that makes to our spiritual mentality and mission. Before turning to this question we will think more about the human experience of exile as well as its significance to the people of God.

The experience of exile

The experience of exile is an all too common one. At any one time there are millions of refugees or exiles living in the world. In 2001 78 per cent of all refugees came from ten areas: Afghanistan, Burma, Burundi, Congo-Kinshasha, Eritrea, Iraq, the Palestinian territories, Somalia and the Sudan. All of them are instantly recognized as being countries rife with instability, much of it continuing (see the Human Rights Website, <www.hrweb.org>). The reason for the existence of most refugees or exiles (and the terms are almost interchangeable) is conflict in their homeland. The difference between a refugee and exile may be that while the exile has been intentionally banished, the refugee has fled as the only way to escape extreme environmental, economic or political disorder. One description of an exile is 'a banished person, compelled by circumstances to reside away from their native land' (*Shorter Oxford English Dictionary*). However, exile may be experienced in a number of ways.

If exile is usually defined by the loss of a familiar environment from which we draw both identity and meaning, it may also be described in psychological terms as well as territorial ones. It may thus be defined as the loss of something psychologically familiar as well as homeland itself. Gordon Mursell in his book *Praying in Exile* describes this psychological loss as a form of exile. Other forms of exile are experienced by the patient who goes into hospital, losing independence, control and the familiar environment of home; the bereaved widow or widower who enters a time defined by acute loss; the person suffering loss of memory on account of a disease like Alzheimer's (Mursell, 2005, p. 6). Some might go even further and say birth itself is a kind of exile, as a baby is thrust out of its cosy lair in the womb to face the challenges and adventures of the world. However, to describe any form of loss as a kind of exile, although having some truth, is to lose the definition of the word. To be an exile is essentially to be forced out of your homeland, to become a stranger in a foreign land and, for the purposes of this book, this must be our basic definition.

Down the years there have been particular communities of exiles whose experience has been powerfully expressed. None more so than the Jews who, having been driven from Judah after the fall of Jerusalem to the Babylonian forces, found themselves settled by an alien river, either the Tigris or Euphrates or possibly that less well-known river that figures in Ezekiel, the Kebar River (Ezekiel 1.3), where they could not rejoice. There the Palmist tells us in words loaded with poignancy and grief:

> By the rivers of Babylon we sat and wept
>   when we remembered Zion.
> There on the poplars we hung our harps,
> for there our captors asked us for songs,
>   our tormentors demanded songs of joy;
>   they said, 'Sing us one of the songs of Zion!'
>
> How can we sing the songs of the LORD
>   while in a foreign land?
>   (Psalm 137.1–4)

If the sense of loss prevented the Jews from singing the Lord's song at first, it may well have been that after some years of getting to grips with how the Lord had led them as well as understanding that he was still with them in exile (as the stories of Daniel and Esther make clear) they came to be able to sing the Lord's song again. What is clear from the understanding of other exiles is that the experience of exile becomes a powerful emotive force, especially in the hearts of the more expressive members of the community, in the lives of poets, writers and musicians. In Greek literature the longing for home is no more powerfully expressed than in the epic poem of Homer, *The Odyssey*, in which Odysseus longs for his home in Greece after being away in the Trojan wars. His longing for Greece and in particular for his homeland, the island of Ithaka, is the thread on which the beads of his adventures are strung. Without the final destination and yearning or nostalgia for his homeland his adventures would lack the tension and emotional drama which makes Homer's work so strong (see Lane Fox, 2005, p. 16). The longing for homeland and the sense of exile has both inspired and transformed the work of artists ever since.

A group of exiles who are almost peerless in their expression of longing for homeland are the Russian exiles or émigrés scattered around Europe and beyond after the Russian Revolution. Few revolutions have created such a group of artists mostly inspired by their longing for their homeland. They had the skill and the resources to express what many exiles have in their hearts. In his last major interview in 1941, the composer Rachmaninov revealed the spiritual connection between this outpouring of emotion and his Russianness. He said,

> 'I am a Russian composer, and the land of my birth has influenced my temperament and outlook. My music is a product of this temperament, and so it is Russian music. I never consciously attempt to write Russian music, or any other kind of music. What I try to do when writing down music is to say simply and directly what is in my heart.'   (quoted by Figes, 2001, p. 543)

Above all it was the memory of the land which inspired him. Figes again says,

> The other source of Rachmaninov's nostalgia was his longing for the Russian land. He yearned for one patch of land in particular: his wife's estate at Ivanovka, five hundred kilometres south-east of Moscow, where he spent his summers from the age of eight, when the Rachmaninov's were forced to sell their own estate.   (Figes, 2001, p. 543)

Eventually this estate came into his own possession through marriage and it was here that he composed almost all his music before 1917. As he later explained,

> 'The Russians feel a stronger tie to the soil than any other nationality. It comes from an instinctive inclination towards quietude, tranquillity, admiration of nature, and perhaps a quest of solitude. It seems to me that every Russian is a hermit.'   (Figes, 2001, p. 544)

Perhaps only the Jews in exile had a greater yearning for their land than the Russians; for the land was integral to the promise of their future and was an inspiration to their faith.

Rachmaninov was one of a constellation of Russian exiles who expressed their longings through their art. Stravinsky, Chagall, Diaghilev, Prokofiev, Solzhenitsyn and Pasternak were others. On the other hand Shostakovich stayed in Stalinist Russia; he was one of the few to remain and retain the ability to create. Exiled from his beloved Russia, Prokofiev wrote,

> 'Because I am a Russian, and that is to say the least suited to be an exile, and therefore to remain myself in a psychological climate that isn't of my race. My compatriots and I carry our country with us. Not all of it, but just enough for it to be faintly painful at first, then increasingly so, until at last it breaks us down altogether . . . I've got to talk to people who are my flesh and blood, so that they can give me something I lack here – their songs, my songs.'
> (Moreux, 1949, p. 9, quoted by Figes, 2001, p. 575)

Few give a better insight into the yearning of the exile, and in the end he returned to Russia explaining with these words why he did so. Likewise Stravinsky made a public show at first of distancing himself from Russia; after all, it had betrayed him – it had become Red Russia. Only later when living in California did he mix almost entirely with Russians, speak Russian, have Russian servants: 'he drank tea in the Russian way, in a glass with jam. He ate his soup from the same spoon with which as a child he had been fed by his baboushka' (Figes, 2001, p. 566). And Chagall, who settled in Nice, where he is especially remembered, came originally from Vitebesk, a border town with Belarus: half Russian, half Jewish. He too testified to the prevailing influence of his childhood home: 'In my pictures there is not one centimetre free from the nostalgia of my native land' (Alexander, 1978, quoted by Figes, 2001, p. 566). In 1944 Chagall wrote a moving tribute in the *New York Times* to his hometown and its influence upon him:

> It is a long time since I saw you, and found myself among your fenced streets. You didn't ask in pain, why I left you for so many years when I loved you. No, you thought: the lad's gone off somewhere in search of brilliant unusual colours to shower like snow or stars on our roofs. But where will he get them from? Why can't he find them near to hand? In your ground I left the graves of my ancestors and scattered stones. I did not live with you and yet there was not a single one of my pictures in which your joys and sorrows were not

reflected. All through these years I had one constant worry: does my native town understand me?

(*New York Times*, 15 February 1944,
quoted by Figes, 2001, p. 567)

Chagall expresses the anxiety of being misunderstood, the pain of even being considered a deserter, the inspiration of his hometown and area, the draw of his ancestors and the shadowy guilt of not being there to suffer with those who lived in his imagination but from whom he was separated by virtue of his vocation. In many ways he expresses what many exiles feel when contemplating those whom they have been forced to leave behind.

We have focused on these Russian exiles, not because they are typical of all exiles, for clearly they are more talented, well resourced and recognized than most, but because with their superior artistic skills they were able to encapsulate for many others the emotions and experience of exile. They expressed longing, nostalgia, grief and lament, recapturing at a distance what inspired them from their home-land. Most exiles are not so talented, nor so recognized for their gifts, nor so well born or well connected. For many exiles their life is bound by poverty, uncertainty, deprivation and sometimes abuse from their new-found compatriots. Nor is it surprising that finding themselves washed up in an alien culture they group together and try to create the culture and conditions to which they are used. Although this is true of almost all immigrants, the exile is in a different category. He or she has been forced to leave, their coming is not a decision of choice to better themselves economically or socially. They are where they are because they have nowhere else to go. In Britain over the generations we have had all types of communities, some exiles, some immigrants from the Empire like the Indians, West Indians and Pakistanis, some now like the Poles who are economic migrants from within the EU who have come in their hundreds of thousands in a few years, and some who are fleeing conflicts in the world.

In Britain there has been an honourable tradition to give asylum to those whose lives are evidently threatened in their home countries. One of the first such waves of asylum-seekers were the Huguenots who came to England in the seventeenth century after the Repeal of the Edict of Nantes (which granted religious toleration to the Protestants in France after the religious wars of the sixteenth century).

xvii

But even before this in Tudor England there were as many as 40,000 aliens living in London. They were described as 'for the most part heretics, fled from other countries' (Leech, 2001, p. 21). Later the Huguenots brought with them a great range of skills as craftsmen, particularly in furniture, lace, weaving and silk. Much of their work at the time adorns the country houses of England (for example, Broughton Hall, Northamptonshire, home of the Montagus). And one Huguenot descendant was to command the British army in the reigns of George II and III (see Whitworth, 1957 and 2006). At the outset the Huguenots, like successive exilic or immigrant communities, settled in the East End of London around Brick Lane. The Huguenots built some thirty-five churches there.

The Huguenots were to be followed by the Jews expelled from central Europe in the nineteenth century in successive waves. By 1800 the number of Jews in London had reached 20,000. After the Russian pogroms following the assassination of Tsar Alexander II in 1881, the liberator of the serfs, the Jewish population had risen to 90 per cent of the population of Whitechapel. They became there the basis of the rag trade and some churches were changed to synagogues. And alongside the influx of Jews from Eastern Europe a new wave of immigration arrived brought by indescribable famine on the doorstep of Britain. By 1851, the year of the great Victorian Census, there were 108,548 Irish residents in London. Some 60,000 Irish moved to London between the years 1841 and 1861 following the failure of the potato harvest in 1846 to 1848. Bringing few skills and next to no resources, they provided labour for the rapidly expanding railway system and were a steady source of supply to the labouring classes of London. These years of great poverty in the East End of London continued well into the twentieth century. The main ambition for new arrivals was, by dint of hard work and good fortune, to leave this holding tank for exiled or immigrant people which was the East End of London. In 1892 Reverend S. G. Reaney wrote about the poverty and tension between the immigrants to the East End and the local residents in the years 1880 to 1890 in a publication called *The Destitute Alien in Great Britain*:

'Those who live and labour in the great East End feel hot and angry at the sight of faces so un-English and the sound of speech so utterly foreign, which crowd pavement and road in Whitechapel,

the Minories, and all the way down Commercial St. and Bethnal
Green.'   (Leech, 2001, p. 64)

The tension between exile or immigrant and the resident population
grew to boiling point with outside political intervention. No more
so than in 1936, when the fascist Moseley held a demonstration with
his black-shirted followers on 4 October in Brick Lane. To the credit
of the East Enders some 250,000 opposed the march, 7,000 police were
deployed and the Battle of Cable Street marked the high-water mark
of racial abuse in the East End in pre-war Britain, stoked by the political ambitions of Moseley who was later arrested in 1940.

All this is to note that exile is a huge social human phenomenon.
In the East End the Irish and the Jews have moved up the social scale,
the East End of London is now more the preserve of the Bengalis,
the West Africans and the Somalis. Church has turned to synagogue,
to church, to mosque, to Hindu temple and now to church again.
And with global movement of people and a growing disparity in wealth
between North and South, it is one of the greatest humanitarian
challenges facing the global North today. As I have said, not every
refugee is an exile, but when an economic migrant is moving
because of necessity and not simply because of choice, it is hard to
say whether or not they can be classed as an exile. We can see that
extreme political or economic imperatives to move are as forceful as
each other, and who is to say that one reason makes someone a more
bona fide exile than another?

I have sought to show in this chapter that exile is an all too common human experience and one that appears to be on the increase
again in the global movements of peoples from East to West and South
to North. Exile, however it is caused, results in the loss of homeland,
the need to reorientate in a foreign land, the hope of peaceful return,
and a further whole gamut of emotions of regret, relief, guilt and
anxiety for those who have been unable 'to get out'. It gives rise to
feelings of longing for the familiar, lament for what is past and the
sheer determination to improve one's lot in the land of one's adoption. Millions have done these things, not least in that country
where a nation has been composed of the people that filed through
Ellis Island, New York, the arrival point for throngs of refugees from
Europe and the Caribbean, who were seeking entry into the United
States. But however hopeful of a new and better life such refugees or

exiles are, they cannot throw off a sense of being in a strange land where they can never be fully understood, where they can never fully be themselves.

Exile is therefore an all too familiar human phenomenon. It is part of most nations' histories, either as recipients of substantial numbers of exiles or as nations which, at one time or another, have seen many of their members forced into exile for longer or shorter periods. But exile has a special meaning and significance to both Jews and Christians and we must now unearth that meaning in our investigation of whether the church or Christian community faces a kind of exile today.

1

Exile and the people of God

There can be no doubt that the theme of exile is integral to the history of the people of God, especially in the Old Testament, where it is one of the major themes. In the New Testament exile is, as we shall see, descriptive of the way the church is to be in the world.

Much of the Old Testament story is taken up with exile. The call of Abraham with which the story begins is a call to go into a kind of exile or at the very least a call to leave the familiar. Abraham was called to go to a place that God would show him (Genesis 12.1ff). To make such a journey required great faith and Abraham was rewarded when God took him outside his tent one night and told him to look up at the starry host, promising him that his descendants would be equally multitudinous. Abraham believed and, as we are told by Paul, this faith was 'reckoned to him a righteousness' (see Genesis 15.6 and Romans 4.1–12). Abraham's faith became the prototype for all saving faith, as Paul argued in Romans, but it was a faith born of a call to leave Ur of the Chaldees and to go to a place that was unfamiliar, which God would show him. The patriarchs settled in this Promised Land but they still regarded themselves as aliens or exiles (Genesis 28.4), so Jacob, like Isaac before him, was encouraged to find a wife not among the Hittite or Canaanite women who surrounded them there but in Paddan Aram where Rebekah his mother came from (see Genesis 27.46—28.9).

Much later Jacob (or Israel), the father of the twelve tribes, now living in Canaan had to leave his home again, because of famine, and go down to Egypt where Joseph his favourite son had risen to become second only to Pharaoh in the realm. The children of Israel were to remain there in Egypt for 450 years where they became enslaved. Undoubtedly this sojourn in an alien land where they lost their liberty was a further form of exile from which they were delivered by the power of God working through Moses. Only after ten plagues culminating in the slaying of the Egyptian firstborn (the

Passover) were the Israelites able to leave and even then they were pursued by the Egyptians as far as the Red Sea in the hope of enslaving them once more. Not for the first time would the people of God return from exile to their homeland. But in the case of the whole Exodus event – the sojourn in Egypt as well as the deliverance from captivity – this experience was not only an historic experience of salvation but also a nation-building exercise of great profundity which formed their vocation for the future. This was the vocation which the Israelites, according to Paul, who stands in the tradition of the great prophets who warned Israel, failed to fulfil (see Romans 9—11).

The vocation of Israel was that they should be a 'light for the nations' (Isaiah 42.6). After all, 'Theirs is the adoption as sons; theirs the divine glory, the covenants, the receiving of the law, the temple worship and the promises. Theirs are the patriarchs, and from them is traced the human ancestry of Christ' (Romans 9.4–5). And yet to a large extent the history or narrative of the Old Testament is a narrative of the Israelites' failure to live out this vocation which they had been given. Only for a short time under the kingship of David and Solomon was the nation a semblance of what it was intended to be, and even David, despite his brilliance and his genuine spirituality, allowed fissures into his family through personal failures which were to prove fatal to the prosperity of his line. After Solomon the kingdom, as prophesied, became divided into Israel and Judah and a path of decline appears to have set in. The 'Early Prophets' of the Jewish Scriptures, comprising Joshua, Judges, Samuel and Kings, chart the rise and fall of the nation under its leaders until it was defeated, first by the Assyrians who overwhelmed and resettled the Northern Kingdom, and then by the Babylonians who destroyed Jerusalem and the Southern Kingdom.

The year 597 BC saw the initial capture of Jerusalem by the forces of King Nebuchadnezzar. Eleven years later, after a fruitless rebellion by King Zedekiah (587–586 BC), the city was utterly destroyed after an appalling siege which is recorded in great vividness and horror in the book of Lamentations. Its opening lines could not be more poignant or sad:

> How deserted lies the city,
>   once so full of people!

> How like a widow is she,
>   who once was great among the nations!
> She who was queen among the provinces
>   has now become a slave
> . . . Among all her lovers
>   there is none to comfort her.
>   (Lamentations 1.1, 2b)

What was once threatened had come about.

The Book of Deuteronomy was perhaps *the* book of theological reflection in the Torah and its tradition was probably only finally settled during the exile itself (Brueggemann, 2002, p. 87). As Brueggemann says,

> The book of Deuteronomy stands as a primal example of the dynamism of the Torah tradition whereby old memories are end-lessly re-presented and re-interpreted, rearticulated, and re-imagined in ways that keep the main claims of faith pertinent and authorita-tive in new circumstances. It is this vitality of the Deuteronomic trad-ition that was a key factor in permitting Israel to flourish even after it lost the conventional supports of temple, monarchy and city in the crises of 587 BC and in the ensuing period of exilic displacement.
>   (Brueggemann, 2002, p. 93)

Deuteronomy was probably completed, scholars suggest, during the exile in Babylon (see Brueggeman, 2002, p. 5, p. 92). The general structure of the book is based around three speeches of Moses preparing the people of Israel for their settlement of the Promised Land after the Exodus. The speeches contain reflection, warning and encouragement. Towards the end of the book Moses says, 'He has declared that he will set you [Israel] in praise, fame and honour high above all the nations he has made and that you will be a people holy to the LORD your God, as he promised' (Deuteronomy 26.19). But with such a privilege came a heavy responsibility. Their responsibility was that they remained true to their calling or vocation, true to Yahweh and the lifestyle of his commandments. This was made abundantly clear in Deuteronomy, for instance where Moses warns that 'if you then become corrupt and make any kind of idol, doing evil in the eyes of the LORD your God and provoking him to anger, I call heaven and earth as witnesses against you this day that you will quickly perish from the land . . . The LORD will scatter [exile] you among the peoples, and only a few of you will survive among the nations to which the LORD will drive you' (Deuteronomy 4.25–27; see the whole passage ending at v. 31). And at the end of the book Moses is both prescient and prophetic when he says,

> 'For I know after my death you are sure to become utterly corrupt and to turn from the way I have commanded you. In days to come, disaster will fall upon you because you will do evil in the sight of the LORD and provoke him to anger by what your hands have made.'
> (Deuteronomy 31.29)

The evidence provided by the books of Kings and Chronicles (representing the royal and Temple traditions respectively) was that they failed their calling and so faced the scattering which was threatened. Despite periods of reform and renewal in Judah, for example under Hezekiah (2 Kings 18ff) and Josiah, in whose reign was discovered the scroll of Deuteronomy in the Temple, which was then implemented (2 Kings 23), the downward spiral of idolatry and unfaithfulness was so ingrained that these reversals did not prevent the final judgement of Judah and Jerusalem. Although delivered from Assyria under whose power Israel succumbed (see 2 Kings 17), Judah in the end fell to Babylon and its exile began. The punishment for failing to live according to the Covenant was the implementation of the threat of exile which was present in Deuteronomy all along, a tradition which would be fully and finally developed in the exile itself. However, before that awful punishment was enacted God sent his servants the prophets to warn his people of impending disaster unless they changed their ways.

The Latter Prophets: messages of judgement and hope

The Latter Prophets in the Jewish Scriptures comprise Isaiah, Jeremiah, Ezekiel and the twelve Minor Prophets. Their prophecies brought judgement, the threat of punishment as well as the hope of restoration. Several of the Minor Prophets are post-exilic (that is, their message is for Judah after its return from Babylon – for instance Haggai, Zechariah, Malachi) but in the three major Latter Prophets – Isaiah, Jeremiah and Ezekiel – we have an unparalleled insight into God's yearning for his people and warning of what lay ahead if they did not change their ways. We shall look, necessarily briefly, at the message of each in turn, beginning with Isaiah.

Isaiah's prophecy may be divided into three parts. The first 39 chapters are generated by Isaiah himself in the context of pre-exilic Jerusalem from 742 to 701 BC (Brueggemann, 2002, p. 161). By this time Judah like her neighbour Israel had more or less abandoned faithfulness to the Torah and the exclusive worship of Yahweh. They had repaid his gifts with abuse, idolatry and injustice. As a result Isaiah, called while worshipping in Solomon's temple in the year that King Uzziah died (see Isaiah 6), came at first with a blistering message of impending judgement. The Lord 'looked for justice, but saw bloodshed; for righteousness, but heard cries of distress' (Isaiah 5.7b). In so-called First Isaiah there is a cascade of rebuke and judgement in these initial 39 chapters, interspersed with glimpses of hope and coming transformation. The prophet therefore laments that 'The Daughter of Zion is left like a shelter in a vineyard, like a hut in a field of melons, like a city under siege' (Isaiah 1.8) and declares that she has neglected justice and faithfulness:

> Woe to those who make unjust laws,
>   to those who issue oppressive decrees,
> to deprive the poor of their rights
>   and withhold justice from the oppressed of my people,
> making widows their prey
>   and robbing the fatherless.
> What will you do on the day of reckoning,
>   when disaster comes from afar?
>
> (Isaiah 10.1–3)

But Isaiah also utters great prophecies of hope. Indeed, 'There will be no more gloom for those who are in distress' for 'the people walking in darkness have seen a great light; on those living in the land of the shadow of death a light has dawned', because a child called 'Wonderful Counsellor, Mighty God, Everlasting Father, Prince of Peace' is coming (Isaiah 9.2ff). So the prediction of judgement is not unrelieved, indeed the hope of restoration is even now planted, and the prophecies of First Isaiah end in King Hezekiah's reign with the avoidance of destruction by the Assyrians. Nevertheless, this proved to be more a deferring of disaster rather than a final escape from it.

5

Alongside Isaiah's judgement on an unrepentant nation, as well as surrounding nations, is one of the most sustained pieces of hopeful prophetic writing in the entire Old Testament. Second Isaiah, which begins at chapter 40, opens a section of prophecy more significant than any other in the Old Testament.

> Comfort, comfort my people, says your God.
> Speak tenderly to Jerusalem
>   and proclaim to her
> that her hard service has been completed,
>   that her sin has been paid for,
> that she has received from the LORD's hand
>   double for all her sins.

These are words of tenderness and restoration to a nation that has suffered exile for her failures and that has renewed her vocation. While in exile Judah has learnt again of the sovereignty of God over all nations (40.15ff), that his concern is with all the nations, not simply Israel, and that his purposes are ever new and fresh (42.8, 9). While in exile a glimpse has been given of a new deliverer who is to come: first, a king who will unwittingly do God's bidding to release Israel from their captivity, Cyrus (Isaiah 45), and then, more profoundly, the Suffering Servant, who will bear the sins of many, going himself into exile that others may be restored (see Isaiah 53). In Second Isaiah God is declared as universal in both love and power; he loves not only wayward Israel but all nations, having purpose for them too. The theme of Isaiah as with the other major prophetic authors is that the displacement of Judah from her land, institutions and ceremony is to be followed by restoration, not in the same way as before, but now caught up in the universal purpose of God for the whole world through the coming of the Messiah. It is a process of displacement and restoration we would do well to hold on to as we try to evaluate the position of the church in Northern Europe today. Last, in Isaiah's final chapters, often called Third Isaiah, the vision is extended yet further with an even more distinctive eschatological flavour. Containing as it does the mandate for the Messiah which Jesus himself used in the synagogue in Nazareth (Isaiah 61.1–3; Luke 4.14–21), the prophecy focuses the listener on the eventual outcome of 'new heavens and a new earth', a new existence full of prosperity and peace for the person whom God prefers, the one 'who is humble and contrite in spirit, and trembles at my word' (Isaiah 65.17ff and 66.2).

The same themes of judgement and hope are equally present in the second great prophetic book connected to the exile, namely that of Jeremiah. Unlike the book of Isaiah, whose prophecies were written over the better part of two centuries, Jeremiah's prophecy is coterminous with his life. Called from a simple background, unlike Isaiah who was of more aristocratic stock, Jeremiah was given strong reassurance at the outset that he had been called to this difficult vocation (see Jeremiah 1.5ff). His calling was a hard one, repeatedly having to tell the court and officials of Judah that unless they radically changed their ways they would face disaster. Appearing on the scene when Assyrian power was waning, around 627 BC and when Babylonian power was gaining strength, he warned that it was not time for complacency but rather a time for fundamental reform. His message was poignantly and memorably summed up by the rebuke that the prophet ascribes to God:

> 'My people have committed two sins:
> They have forsaken me,
>   the spring of living water,
> and have dug their own cisterns,
>   broken cisterns that cannot hold water.'
>
> (2.13)

Consequently they faced disaster from the north (4.5ff and 23ff; 6.1c). His prophecies were relentlessly gloomy but true. He hid a linen belt in a rock crevice until it was useless and heard that Judah likewise was irretrievably spoilt (Jeremiah 13.1–11). He went to the potter's house and observed him throwing pots, and then heard the word that God was likewise free to do whatever he wished with the house of Israel (Jeremiah 18.1–10). For his pains, Jeremiah was beaten and imprisoned by the presiding priest in the Temple (Jeremiah 20) with the result that he mourned the day of his birth, so difficult was his task (20.14). Jeremiah inveighed against the last kings of Judah, Jehoiakim and Zedekiah, calling the former king, who burnt his prophecies, 'a broken pot' (36.27 and 22.28) and suffering the indignity of being thrown into a cistern by the latter (38.4ff). For confronting faithfully the rulers of Judah with their faithlessness and their need to reform, Jeremiah faced continual danger and opprobrium from the country's rulers until the disaster he had all along prophesied came about.

But alongside the prophecies of judgement were many of hope too. Like Isaiah these prophecies of hope punctuate the otherwise unremitting, bleak landscape. In the future, Jeremiah prophesies, the Lord will raise up

'to David a righteous Branch,
a King who will reign wisely
and do what is just and right in the land.
In his days Judah will be saved
and Israel will live in safety.
This is the name by which he will be called:
The LORD Our Righteousness.'
(23.5, 6; see also 33.15, 16)

The exile and captivity will have an end, after lasting for seventy years (25.12–14). Jeremiah bought a field in Anathoth from his cousin during the siege of Jerusalem as a sign of hope for the future (32.1ff). Furthermore he wrote a famous letter to the exiles about how they were to live in exile, praying for their captors, building houses and planting gardens and crops, for they had a hope and a future (29.11). That hope would find its fulfilment in a new covenant in which God promised to 'cleanse them from all the sin they have committed against me', and to 'heal my people and . . . let them enjoy abundant peace and security' (33.8, 6b). So once again the severe prophecies of judgement were mingled always with hope and restoration. We could say therefore that judgement was always God's second-last word!

The last of the great exilic prophets is Ezekiel, perhaps the most unusual of the three. Whereas Jeremiah never accompanied the exiles into Babylon, eventually being forced against his will to go down to Egypt instead (see Jeremiah 42, 43), Ezekiel was the prophet who helped the exiles to understand their past and reimagine their future while living among them in exile itself. The book of Ezekiel divides into two parts: chapters 1—24, taken up with impending judgement of Jerusalem, and the second part, chapters 25—48, which anticipates the restoration of Jerusalem and specifically the worship in the Temple (see Brueggemann, 2002, p. 192). Ezekiel himself appears to have been deported from Jerusalem in the first group of exiles and

8

while in the land of the Chaldeans by the river Kebar he received his call to be a prophet (see Ezekiel 1—3). The early chapters of the prophecy anticipate the destruction of the city. Ezekiel symbolized, with prophetic drama, the final siege of Jerusalem by lying on his left side for 390 days before a picture of the city on a clay tablet (Ezekiel 4.5), each day representing a year of the nation's sin. The eventual judgement of the city is terrible: a third dying by famine or disease; a third by the sword and a third scattered to the winds (5.12). And in the midst of this catastrophe was the destruction of the Temple preceded by the glory of God leaving it. The presence of the Lord manifested by the cherubim, themselves connected to the mysterious wheels first seen by the prophet at his call by the River Kebar, left the Temple by the East gate leaving it vulnerable to destruction (10.9–22). The exiles were not to mourn for the passing of Jerusalem, their delight, as Ezekiel himself was not to mourn the passing of his wife, the delight of his eyes (chapter 24). But the prophet would remain silent because of his wife's death until he heard the news that the city had indeed fallen (twelve years after the beginning of their exile) and then he would speak again, this time a message of hope and reassurance (see 33.21, 22). But the destruction of Jerusalem was necessary because 'the devastation' of Jerusalem 'constitutes the vigorous reassertion of YHWH's holiness for all to see' (Brueggemann, 2002, p. 197).

The second part of Ezekiel's prophecy is irradiated with hope. And just as the glory of the Lord leaving the Temple lies at the heart of Jerusalem's fate, so the renewal of the Temple and its worship lies at the centre of Jerusalem and her people's restoration. The climax of the message of hope may be found both in the new Covenant which is coming and the new Temple worship which will be restored. 'I will give you a new heart and put a new spirit in you; I will remove from you your heart of stone and give you a heart of flesh,' prophesied Ezekiel (36.26) and 'I will put breath in [these dry bones], and you will come to life' (see 37.4ff). The nation would be re-established as one nation in Israel and reconnected with the land (37.22, 24). And Ezekiel saw in a vision, similar again to the original vision by the River Kebar, that the Temple would become once more the centre of their worship and from it a stream of life-giving water would flow for the healing of the nations (see 43.4, 5 and 47.1ff).

So through each of these three great prophecies twin themes run: first judgement, which would inevitably come upon an unrepentant

Judah and upon her capital city Jerusalem and part of that punishment or judgement would be her people being carried into exile; but this was not the final action of God for it would be followed by (that other great prophetic theme) the restoration of Israel (Judah), arising from this remnant of the nation transported to Babylon, following a time in which they came to understand their past and reimagine their future. And they would do all this while living by the very rivers of Babylon where they had sat down and wept, and where they had found that they could no longer sing the Lord's song.

Besides these great prophets, others would come to the nation's aid both to inspire faithfulness in exile itself, as Daniel and Esther did, and to help with the task of rebuilding Jerusalem and the state when the exiles eventually arrived back to a destroyed and humiliated land. Leaders and prophets such as Nehemiah and Ezra, Haggai and Zechariah were required to provide both the leadership and inspiration, to bring the vision of these great Latter Prophets into being. But the truth is that the underlying symbols and hopes present in the prophecies of Isaiah, Jeremiah and Ezekiel would not be properly fulfilled until the arrival of the Messiah and the New Covenant which he came to inaugurate. But what is undeniable is that the events of the exile loom large in the story of the Old Testament and their lessons cannot be neglected.

And as we go on to consider, later in this book, whether the church in Britain faces a kind of exile, we too must hold onto the fact that the people of Israel displaced in Babylon without their land, their ceremonies, their previous rhythm of worship, had both to understand their past (what had happened and where they had gone wrong) and also to reimagine their future. Just as this process of reinterpretation, reimagination and rearticulation was so vital to gaining a new vision for Israel with the help of the prophetic word during those years in Babylon, so the church in Britain, facing arguably another kind of dispossession, must go through a similar process to understand its shape and mission for the future.

Exile and the New Testament

Exile as a continuing theme runs through much of the Old Testament and it likewise is strongly present in the theology and the experience of the New Testament. To start with the theology first: exile lies at the heart of the Christian message of redemption.

> At the epicentre of Christian faith is the conviction that God embraced exile in order to rescue us from ours, that God became homeless in order to bring all of us home, and that in the life and death of resurrection of Jesus we are not only offered a paradigm for finding hope and meaning in our own journeys of exile, but also set free to embrace and make our own the vision of a new cosmos which he came to proclaim. (Mursell, 2005, p. 75)

Or if we go back to Genesis we see the effects of the Fall: a man and a woman banished (exiled) from Paradise for their disobedience, with God consequently setting at its entrance angels with flaming swords preventing any return to the tree of life (Genesis 3.24). But then a second Adam comes and makes the cross (his sacrificial death: a temporary exile from the Father's love) into a new tree of life so that those who have been exiled may return. What Adam had done, Jesus has undone, as Paul so majestically explains in Romans: 'For if the many died by the trespass of the one man, how much more did God's grace and the gift that came by the grace of the one man, Jesus Christ, overflow to the many!' (Romans 5.15, but see the whole section from 5.15–21). In his redemptive work Jesus tasted the depth of his exile from the Father when he cried out, 'My God, my God, why have you forsaken me?' (Mark 15.34b). He therefore bore our exile that we might find our true home, and in so doing he reopened the way to the tree of life. In the Book of Revelation John describes a scene in which all exile is ended in breathtaking terms:

> Then the angel showed me the river of the water of life, as clear as crystal, flowing from the throne of God and of the Lamb down the middle of the great street of the city. On each side of the river stood the tree of life, bearing twelve crops of fruit, yielding its fruit every month. And the leaves of the tree are for the healing of the nations. No longer will there be any curse. The throne of God and of the Lamb will be in the city, and his servants will serve him. They will see his face, and his name will be on their foreheads. There will be no more night. They will not need the light of a lamp or the light of the sun, for the Lord God will give them light. And they will reign for ever and ever. (Revelation 22.1–5)

This visionary description is indeed the end of all exile. But alongside this description, which is a fundamental part of New Testament theology, is also New Testament experience: while Jesus proclaimed an ultimate end of exile he also made it clear that to be a friend of his was to be an enemy of the world, and therefore to be an exile in it. We must explore this paradox a little further to make sense of it.

First, we must begin by retracing our steps a little and sketch in some history. In my description of exile in the Old Testament I ended with Israel in Babylon being reformed through the great prophetic words of Second Isaiah, Jeremiah and Ezekiel and being further encouraged by the examples of Daniel and Esther, and in Daniel's case by his visionary prophecy too, which stretched well into the future, seeing the shape of international relations in centuries to come (see Daniel 7 and 8). The walls of Jerusalem were rebuilt under Nehemiah's leadership; the Temple was rebuilt, although it was nothing like the great wonder of the world which Solomon had built earlier. And until the supremacy of Greece in the region, the newly restored, post-exile Israel existed within a Persian sphere of influence. However, with the advent of Alexander the Great around 330 BC Israel had new rulers, the Ptolemies and the Seleucids, who successively governed her. The Ptolemies, whose original power base was in Egypt, were displaced by the Seleucids in 198 BC at the battle of Panenon. The Seleucids proved less accommodating rulers towards the Jews, and under Antiochus IV a full-scale repression of Jewish religious observance and customs came about. He robbed the Temple to pay for his wars with Egypt and Rome; he banned circumcision and Sabbath-keeping and even the reading of the Torah. Finally he erected a statue of the pagan deity Zeus in the Temple to be worshipped. It was this that triggered the revolt of the Jews led by Judas Maccabeus in 165 BC and the eventual rededication of the Temple to God three years later. The annual Jewish feast of Hanukkah is celebrated to mark the restoration of the Temple. Gradually Greek power in the region waned until Pompey's armies gained the upper hand and Israel passed into Roman control. It was now that new communities such as the Qumran community by the Dead Sea (believed by many scholars to be Essenes) came together to maintain, in another form of exile based on purity and asceticism, the longings of Judaism. This early Jewish monastic-style movement would later be copied in Christendom (see Wright, 1992, p. 203). Likewise at a similar time the Pharisees emerged as a kind of religious resistance movement bent on maintaining the purity of Judaism over against collusion with Rome.

As we trace what happened to Israel in the four centuries prior to the arrival of Jesus it is not surprising that many thought that the exile which had begun in Babylon had not really ended. As Tom Wright writes,

> Babylon had taken people into captivity; Babylon fell, and the people returned. But in Jesus' day many, if not most, Jews regarded the exile as still continuing. The people had returned in a geographical sense, but the great prophecies of restoration had not yet come true. What was Israel to do? Why, to repent of the sin which had driven her into exile and to return to Yнwн with all her heart.
>
> (Wright, 1996, p. 126)

So when Jesus emerged, after the dramatic ministry of John the Baptist and John's call to repentance, preaching the message of the Kingdom, the end of exile was offered in a very profound sense. To belong to this Kingdom of God and to be subject to the Galilean preacher from Nazareth was in a very deep sense to end one exile and yet to begin another. In belonging to this Kingdom through faith in Jesus of Nazareth a spiritual exile had ended, all the promises of the three great prophets were fulfilled and the individual entered into the New Covenant. Indeed all who believe are brought near to the God and Father of Jesus in the greatest possible intimacy through the Spirit and are no longer strangers or alienated (see the message to the Ephesians especially 2.11ff). But to belong to this Kingdom and Covenant was at the same time to become an alien, stranger and exile in the world, and this quickly became the experience of Christians in the period of Jesus' ministry and subsequently.

Jesus never promised his followers an easy time – in fact he repeatedly warned them in his teaching that they would face a hostile response from family, friends and community alike. He said, 'You must be on your guard. You will be handed over to the local councils and flogged in the synagogues. On account of me you will stand before governors and kings as witnesses to them.' He went on to say that commitment to him would bring a kind of civil war into human society: 'Brother will betray brother to death, and a father his child.' In other words he projected the bleak prospect of persecution by civil authorities, antipathy from family members, betrayal by friends and the daily requirement of taking up your cross (Mark 13.9–13; see also Luke 12.11, 12; 21.12–19; Matthew 10.17–23; 24.9).

Likewise in John's writings Jesus spoke repeatedly of enmity between the world and his disciples. The world in John's writings is human society organized without reference to God in which earthly values dominate (see John 15.18–20; 16.33; 17.14, 15). What Jesus spoke about in his lifetime came about soon after his ascension. Persecution or an experience of exile came swiftly upon the church.

The persecution of the church in the Apostolic era

The trial and crucifixion of Jesus inaugurated a persecution of his followers. The Apostles were locked in an upper room after Jesus' crucifixion 'for fear of the Jews' (John 20.19). The authorities were at pains to prevent any rumours about Jesus' resurrection, which he himself had predicted, so they had posted a guard at the garden tomb (Matthew 27.62ff). Soon after Pentecost further intimidation and persecution of the Apostles began. Peter and John were arrested following the healing of the crippled beggar at the Gate Beautiful and warned not to speak in the name of Jesus (Acts 4.1–21). Again the Apostles were arrested and eventually appeared before the Sanhedrin. Only Gamaliel's sage and shrewd advice that the Apostles be left well alone because 'If [their teaching] is from God, you will not be able to stop these men; you will only find yourselves fighting against God' (Acts 5.38, 39) saved them from a worse fate. Nevertheless the persecution intensified: Stephen was stoned to death and Paul began his persecution of the Christian communities outside Jerusalem. But on the road to Damascus all that was to change. Paul, now an Apostle, preacher and church planter, became the target of intense hatred from some Jewish quarters (see Acts 22.30, 31; 22.22; 25.11; 26.4–23). The gospel he preached provoked numerous Jewish congregations to violent persecution of him and his colleagues (Acts 14.19; 17.5ff). And likewise pagan vested interests were challenged by his evangelism with resulting violence against him (see his reception in Philippi, Acts 16.22–24, and Ephesus, Acts 19.23ff).

In the end Paul himself was arrested in Jerusalem by the Roman authorities to prevent him falling into the hands of Jewish extremists (Acts 21.33ff). He was transferred from Jerusalem to Caesarea where he faced trial or investigation by the Roman governor (Acts 23.23ff). Felix's investigation of Paul was swayed by both his wife Drusilla's Jewish origin and his own desire for a bribe (Acts 24.24,

26). When no money was forthcoming, Paul was left to languish in gaol for two more years until at a subsequent trial before the new Roman governor Festus he appealed to Caesar as a Roman citizen (Acts 25.10, 11). If on the one hand his appeal was the way for the Apostle to arrive at the capital city of the Roman Empire it was also a new and significant turning point in the imperial/Christian relations. Accompanying Paul to Rome would be a letter outlining the charges against Paul which he must answer before an imperial court. But Festus was at a loss to know what to write to the Emperor Claudius (Acts 25.23ff). So Festus tells King Agrippa who was visiting him in Caesarea,

> 'I found he had done nothing deserving of death, but because he made his appeal to the Emperor I decided to send him to Rome. But I have nothing definite to write to His Majesty about him. Therefore I have brought him before all of you, and especially before you, King Agrippa, so that as a result of this investigation I may have something to write.'
> (Acts 25.25–26)

In fact they came to the conclusion that there was no charge to answer so something must have been fabricated for the letter. We do not know what Festus put in his letter but we do know that the arrival of 'the Way', or Christians, in Rome began a struggle that lasted around two hundred and fifty years between the Roman authorities throughout the Empire and this new religion that revolved around the following of one 'Chrestus', as Claudius' secretary Suetonius called Jesus. (It's interesting to note that Suetonius later wrote, 'Since the Jews constantly made disturbances at the instigation of Chrestus, he [Claudius] expelled them from Rome' (Stevenson and Frend, 1975 p. 1). For around two hundred and fifty years pagan Rome was at first irritated, then 'entertained' in the games, next challenged, then concerned and finally overwhelmed by this little known part-Jewish, part-Gentile sect called 'the Way'. And all the while they wrote of themselves and believed themselves to be exiles.

When Peter – who had been imprisoned on numerous occasions in Jerusalem and sometimes had also been miraculously set free, and who, like Paul, had ended up in Rome during the Emperor Nero's notorious reign – wrote to the Christians scattered in Pontus, Galatia, Cappadocia, Asia and Bithynia, he addressed them as 'strangers [sojourners, exiles] in the world' (1 Peter 1.1). And that is how they

truly regarded themselves. For in the *Epistle to Diognetus*, the author
wrote: (1st half of Second Century)

> For Christians are distinguished from other men neither by country,
> nor language, nor the customs which they observe for they neither
> inhabit cities of their own, nor employ a particular form of speech,
> nor lead a life which is marked out by any singularity . . . They dwell
> in their own countries but simply as sojourners. As citizens, they share
> in all things with others, and yet endure all things as if foreigners.
> Every foreign land is to them as their native country and every land
> of their birth as a land of strangers . . . To sum it all in one word: what
> the soul is in the body, that are Christians in the world. The soul is
> dispersed through all the members of the body and Christians are
> scattered through all the cities of the world. The soul dwells in the
> body, yet it is not of the body; and Christians dwell in the world yet
> are not of the world.   (Roberts and Donaldson, 1975, pp. 26, 27)

The writer of the *Epistle to Diognetus* appreciated that Christians
lived as strangers, sojourners and exiles in the world. They were
spread throughout the known world but never at home in any place:
paradoxically at home both everywhere and nowhere.

In this chapter we have had to dig relatively deeply into the theme
of exile in the Scriptures and in the story of God's people on earth
spread over the past five thousand years since the call of Abraham.
It is a theme never far from God's people either in the Old or New
Testament. The Israelites were never to forget that they were sprung
from 'a wandering Aramaean' (Deuteronomy 26.5), and that they were
the descendants of refugees; when they did forget they were in spiritual danger. They were called to a faith journey which resembled that
of a wandering exile seeking home. Abraham was promised a land
which was God's gift to him and his descendants. But before they
were established in the land the people suffered a further exile, this
time in Egypt, until eventually delivered by God's mighty power and
formed into a nation through Moses and the giving of the Torah
during their further wanderings in the desert. Although subsequently
resettled in the Promised Land in the days of Joshua and subsequent
leaders, the warning was always there that if the nation proved
faithless to the Covenant and the call of YHWH then they would
suffer exile. This is exactly what came about despite the further warnings of many prophets. A power from the North came and destroyed

16

their institutions, took their land and carried the people into exile, the Northern Kingdom having been previously destroyed by the Assyrians. With the judgement came also the hope of restoration but with the expectation of re-understanding their role in the region and re-understanding the God who had called them.

Despite their resettlement under the influence of a foreign ruler, Cyrus, a sense of exile persisted. The institutions were never what they had been, foreign domination only changed with regard to who the rulers were: first Greek Ptolemies, then Greek Seleucids and then finally Rome governed them. Their rule spread out over nearly four hundred years. Then a Galilean preacher and healer emerged who preached about a new Kingdom. Many believed that exile and national humiliation would end with him and that he would deliver Israel. But his life appeared to end in utter degradation, abandonment – exile of a different kind – and utter dereliction. Until, that is, his followers claimed that he had risen from the dead. Soon his followers grew in number, inspired by a new reality of their leader's presence within them and between them. They spread all over the Roman world and beyond and they were marked, among other things, by a sense of exile. It seems that the vocation of God's people has always been wrapped up in exile in one way or another. The task for us now is to discover in what way particularly the church in Britain today is in exile and how we should live as such, purposefully and effectively, knowing that this is nothing strange or novel.

through the Holy Spirit. (Acts 2).

2

The church in Britain facing exile today

There are four reasons generally speaking why the church in Britain may be facing a new kind of exile: the building of a secular and pluralist state; a change in culture and its underlying philosophical presuppositions; the erosion of Christendom with its church–state links being further dismantled; and a reduction in the number of people who regularly worship in church. None of these reasons are self-contained, but they spill over into each other, creating the conditions for exile.

In one sense Christians, when truest to their calling, have always felt themselves to be in exile, seeking a home in heaven and having no abiding city here and this is evident in every generation. But for centuries the existence of Christendom (i.e. the existence of a state church and Christian government) often masked the reality of this exile. In the twenty-first century the mask has almost slipped off and the church must now face a far more bracing and challenging climate in which it must reassess its role, re-understand its vocation and above all know more deeply the God who has called it and sent it out in mission to the world. To understand where we are we must trace briefly where we have come from.

The twentieth century produced four massive periods of turbulence and challenge. The first period was the First World War, which was in large part started by Prussian militarism. This militarism had developed over the previous two hundred years. It was further strengthened by the encirclement of Germany by Britain, France and Russia at the beginning of the twentieth century. Prussian militarism was only defeated through unimaginable loss of life on all sides in the trench warfare of 1914 to 1918 so vividly portrayed by the novel *Birdsong* by Sebastian Faulks or the satirical play *Oh! What a Lovely*

War by Charles Chilton (Stevenson, 2004, p. 592). However, the concluding peace, hammered out in the Treaty of Versailles 1919, led to widespread resentment in Germany. Soon after the end of the war the great economic turbulence in capital markets, industry and employment throughout Western societies in the late 1920s created conditions in Germany for resentment to be turned into revenge. In Germany and Italy this instability proved a fertile breeding ground for the rise of fascism, and made possible rearmament on a grand scale linked to aggressive foreign policies. Soon the results of this aggressive stance became clear, with the occupation of Austria and Czechoslovakia by German forces and of Abyssinia (Ethiopia) and North Africa by the Italians. The invasion of Poland in 1939 precipitated the start of the second great challenge to liberal democracies, the Second World War. Differentiated from the First World War by massive civilian casualties, atrocities fuelled by racism committed by the Nazis (and by the Russians against the Poles in the opening stages of the war, especially the destruction of the Polish officer class in Katyn woods) and the holocaust of European Jews, it also exhausted the main participants. Germany lay in ruins, Britain was exhausted and in deep debt, France enfeebled and to a certain extent divided.

The third challenge to the liberal democracies of Western Europe and the United States in the aftermath of the war was the stand off between the Communist East and democratic West which turned into the cold war. The final challenge, with which we are currently living, crystallized on 11 September 2001 ('9/11'), when the Twin Towers of the World Trade Center in New York were destroyed by terrorist attack orchestrated by al-Qaeda. Many suggest this challenge will last at least a generation.

Like very many families mine has been involved to a greater or lesser extent with each of these conflicts: my grandfather was a soldier briefly on the Western Front and then with General Allenby's army in Egypt and Palestine; my father was also a soldier in North Africa and Italy, serving under General Alexander in the Second World War; my family lived in Berlin at the height of the cold war from 1961 to 1963 (including Kennedy's famous visit in the summer of 1963); and my daughter watched from a roof in Manhattan as the Twin Towers burned and fell on 9/11, while she was staying with my brother-in-law. Each saw a part of these epoch-making events.

Why the potted history? Because to comprehend what has happened to the church in Britain we must recall or remember the social, economic and cultural background of the society from which the church is drawn. In particular we must appreciate what was happening in those years preceding the great years of social change which occurred in the mid 1960s.

The 1950s were a kind of grey Indian summer. The values for which the nation had fought persisted, but below the surface the conditions and desire for change were emerging. Exhausted by the war, the country began to dispose of its Empire. At its height some 440 million people lived under its aegis (Ferguson, 2004, p. 240), but by the mid 1960s most of the empire had been granted independence. Immigration to Britain began with the arrival of West Indians on the ship SS *Empire Windrush* in 1948, as Commonwealth citizens sought new futures in the 'mother country', taking up menial jobs in the cities where too often their reception was anything but welcoming. Soon the immigration would involve both the Indian subcontinent and Africa. The beginnings of a pluralist society were laid.

In the 1950s a mixture of greyness and hope struggled for ascendancy. Rationing was still in force and goods were on the whole dreary. It remained a relatively hard time as people sought to get back on their feet after the war. Nevertheless there was also real intellectual and cultural advance. W. H. Auden, T. S. Eliot, J. R. R. Tolkien and C. S. Lewis were writing. Basil Spence's architecture, Piper's glass; Sutherland's art and Benjamin Britten's operas broke new ground in the visual and performing arts. Playwrights such as Osborne, Beckett and later Pinter were among those involved in a new kind of theatre, which searched for meaning and significance in a world where human life was increasingly regarded as inherently meaningless. And at the same time churchgoing remained high and the Haringey Crusades, led by Billy Graham, were full every night and even extended. Parts of society looked in retrospect like a moth trying to escape a chrysalis in which the church was naturally and too frequently associated only with the conventional. By the time of the mid 1960s a desire to throw off old inhibitions had arrived, a revolution of manners was beginning and it is not an exaggeration to say that the church in Britain faced the biggest challenge since the fifth century. How was this so? The challenge came on four fronts and developed out of movements rumbling just below the surface in the late 1950s and early 1960s.

The growth of a pluralist, secular society

Pluralist Britain was kick-started by immigration, developed further by a new culture in the 1960s and made possible by world travel, economic success and gradual globalization. Immigration has increased steadily since the 1950s. It is not to be feared or regretted but it should be understood. Its consequences for Britain are irreversible.

Soon after the Second World War the government encouraged labour from the West Indies and the Indian subcontinent to fill menial jobs in transport and the newly formed NHS, which returning soldiers were not eager to do. By 1954 some 40,000 immigrants had arrived and this was set to increase to 136,000 by 1961 (Horne, 1989, p. 422). Total immigration from Commonwealth countries was set to reach 350,000 by the mid 1960s (Horne, 1989, p. 422). Those from the Indian subcontinent were mostly Hindu and Muslim, while those from the Caribbean, East and West Africa were generally Christian. Today, half the worshipping Christians in London are black, from Africa or the West Indies, and there are now some 1.6 million Muslims in Britain, half of whom are children (*The Times*, 13 September 2007, feature article). Immigration has created the pluralist society in which the state rightly seeks to ensure opportunities and fair treatment for all. The Race Relation bills were passed in the 1960s and culminated in the benchmark Race Relations Act of 1976. In addition, although the act of worship in schools was to be generally Christian, as stipulated by the Butler Education Act 1944 and renewed by later education acts, religious education now included lessons on all the major faiths. So from a position at the beginning of the twentieth century in which the Christian faith, alone of all religions and creeds in Britain, was identified with the state, the state now took on the role of a kind of religious regulator, ensuring space for the faiths of each of the religious communities present within the state. In so doing the government appeared to become more secular in tone. As far as government was concerned, the religious sphere of national life came to be regarded as public space for faith.

Indeed, in the wake of 9/11 the British government tried to take active steps to prevent the rise to, and incitement of, religious hatred. The most recent example of this was the Incitement to Racial and Religious Hatred Bill, whose political background was the potential growth of religious hatred following 9/11, and the possible resulting religious provocation aimed at the Muslim community. In some of its clauses the Bill sought to make religious provocation a criminal offence. However, the government lost a clause in the Bill by *one* vote following an amendment by the House of Lords which stated that only an intentional as opposed to unwitting provocation was culpable. This occurred on 31 January 2006 (the then Prime Minister, Tony Blair, being told by his Chief Whip that his presence was not needed), following a strong campaign against this section of the Bill by some Christians, who thought it might be used against them for preaching the unique claims of Christ to be the Son of God, as well as by comedians such as Stephen Fry and Rowan Atkinson, who saw it as an erosion of free speech, and by lawyers, who felt these offences were adequately covered by other laws. However, it was a clear case of a government seeking to regulate religious pluralism and relations between faiths.

The notion of affording respect to all religious groups as well as religious toleration is strongly held by most Christians. Indeed in Bath where I live there has been a recent attack on a mosque, in which shoes and clothes taken off for prayer were urinated on by intruders; this brought a letter of condemnation and sympathy from a leading Christian minister writing on behalf other Christian leaders in the city. Although the majority of Muslims share the same notion of wanting religious toleration there is, at least in some mosques in Britain, a growth of religious extremism.

Pluralism is a fact of British society and is linked to the huge social, religious and ethnic mix that exists, especially in our cities; some London schools have pupils of as many as thirty different nationalities. But pluralism is not only the existence of many religions, faiths, creeds, philosophies and cultures in society; in the liberal modern mind it is connected to a sense of there being an *equal value* between them: that is, that they are of equal merit, truth and worth. This does not sit easily with the unique claims of Christianity, depending as they do on the incarnation and the consequent uniqueness of Jesus. (Nor, for that matter, does it sit well with the unique claims of some other faiths, such as those found in Judaism and Islam.) Liberal theology, which seeks to find a common minimum of faith between religions, often insists that divisive teachings be dropped, thereby creating a kind of inoffensive religious mix which underpins the existence of pluralism without distinguishing between faiths or creeds. The premise of such pluralistic religious or philosophical thought is that each faith is as valid as the other and none is more truthful, a point we shall return to later. That has the appearance of humility, as it is inoffensive and helps community relations in mixed areas of race in religion. But there are some, not least the Chief Rabbi Jonathan Sacks, who are calling for an end to such expressions of pluralism. And although on the ground robust debate and dialogue between faiths should be encouraged, nevertheless government in our pluralist and multi-cultural society is bound, in the interests of community relations, to arbitrate between the claims of different faith groups, making all subject to the law of Parliament. As already said, government in a pluralistic society seeks to regulate relations between communities and pass laws to enable relations between the faiths to happen fruitfully. So in the past sixty years since the beginning of serious immigration to this country from faith communities other than the Judeo-Christian (e.g. Huguenots in the seventeenth and Jewish immigration in the nineteenth and twentieth centuries), government has inevitably to govern in the interest of all the population and at a time when many in Britain have also become increasingly secular.

Secularization is itself a large study which we can only dip into here, and finding an agreed definition of it is not wholly easy. By and large it can be seen as a process beginning with the loss of temporal power by the church from the mid seventeenth century in Europe (e.g. the Peace of Westphalia ending the Thirty Years' Wars gave power previously held by the church to secular, i.e. non-church-appointed, rulers), and continuing through the growth of rationalism. Thus secularism can be described as the loss of religious consciousness and significance in state and community life. Such a movement has been given rapid stimulation in the past hundred years both by scientific rationalism and the growth of pluralism. It means that Christianity which hitherto occupied public space becomes increasingly a private faith in a competing market of belief (see the work of the socio-logist Berger, himself a follower of Weber). Once again government and public bodies become secular, their aim being to legislate without regard to religious significance. An obvious example of this would be the 1967 Abortion Act which upheld the right of women to choose, and sought to bring to an end the dangers of backstreet abortion (powerfully depicted in the film *Vera Drake* with Imelda Staunton playing Vera Drake, a backstreet abortionist, in an Oscar-nominated performance), but it gave no rights to the unborn of sixteen weeks or less, healthy or unhealthy. It was a utilitarian piece of legislation which sought safety for women, but ended in allowing many more abortions than its sponsors had intended. However, what the secular movement – which had also powerfully permeated the Christian faith, for example in the works of Bishop John Robinson and Harvey Cox – could not have envisaged was that twenty years later in the 1990s religion or 'spirituality' would make a remarkable comeback.

In brief, the movements of pluralism and secularism have had a massive effect in redefining the position and the role of Christian faith and the church in public life, turning what hitherto had been generally accepted as public truth (Christianity) and a public institution (the church) into something either private and or much more restricted in significance (apart from very rare occasions such as the funerals of Princess Diana and of Queen Elizabeth the Queen Mother). On the one hand the position of both Christian faith and the church has changed in society fundamentally, but on the other hand a brand new type of opportunity for mission in a new climate of 'spirituality' has arisen which has not been here before and which must now be welcomed and seized. Understandably the post-war and wartime generation are taking a bit of time getting used to this. Intimately connected to the growth of pluralism and secularism was, in the 1960s, a more widespread change of culture.

A change of culture

Culture is the result of many phenomena working together: these are economic, social, scientific and philosophical and religious. It seems many of these forces converged together in the mid 1960s. Conventions which themselves had been based on religious perceptions were first questioned and then overthrown in a social revolution unseen in Europe since the French Revolution. After the grey 1950s, colour and possibilities returned. As British Prime Minister Macmillan proclaimed in 1957, 'You have never had it so good' (Macmillan in 1957 in a speech in Bedford). Fashions changed, as they do, and the miniskirt was in, the pill was discovered, abortions became easier, the Lord Chamberlain's censorship of London theatres ended, broadcasting standards were liberalized, the Wolfenden Report on Homosexual Offences and Prostitution (1957) was already gathering dust and in 1967 homosexual acts between consenting adults over 21 was decriminalized. Pop culture was born with the Rolling Stones and the Beatles. Satisfaction could be temporarily tasted with dope, and the 'Summer of Love' (1967) and John Lennon's 'Imagine' found a more than ready audience in those opposed to the Vietnam War. Student revolution and demand for change on the streets of Paris and London and the campuses of the United States were commonplace, linking desires for civil rights and international peace. In 1965 the then Home Secretary Roy Jenkins said that it was time for the state to do less to restrict personal freedom (Jenkins, 1991, p. 180) and that is what happened. A change in social habits and a growth in wealth after the stringent 1950s occurred with bewildering speed.

For someone like me from a conventional background these were heady days. One year I was in Paris protesting with French students against the reoccupation of Prague by Soviet forces after the Prague Spring; the next I was on Boston Common in the United States where peace demos, dope and love mixed together in a new cocktail a year after the assassination of the great Martin Luther King, whose dream of a new society, equal and free for black and white, was also intoxicating. You could say as Wordsworth did of the opening of the French Revolution, 'Bliss was it in that dawn to be alive, but to be young was very heaven!' (*The Prelude*). The conjunction of change (on a massive cultural scale) and youth is exhilarating, as the great poet said – but the French Revolution led to the Terror. What is the cost of the social revolution in the West? If Zhou Enlai, the Chinese Premier, said in 1951 that it was too soon to judge the effects of the French Revolution, then the social revolution begun in the 1960s has only just begun to run its course and it is much too soon to judge its effects; however, we can draw some tentative conclusions.

Cultural change is either preceded by or accredited by more fundamental shifts in values which are themselves linked to philosophic or religious perceptions. The fact is that philosophical outlook was changing in the 1960s too. The influential non-Christian philosopher Bertrand Russell (see his *Why I Am Not a Christian*) published his incisive and readable *History of Western Philosophy* in 1945; it remains a classic even though it ends before the new so-called postmodern philosophy came into existence. Nevertheless in his penultimate chapter Russell warns of the dangers of thought becoming unrelated to fact and objective truths. He says in a prescient kind

of way of John Dewey (a leading late nineteenth-century US philosopher who held that all truth or fact is predicated on belief), that

> The concept of 'truth' as something dependent upon facts largely out-
> side of human control has been one of the ways in which philosophy
> hitherto has inculcated the necessary element of humility. When this
> check upon pride is removed, a further step is taken on the road to-
> wards a certain kind of madness – the intoxication of power which
> invaded philosophy with Fichte, and to which modern men, whether
> philosophers or not are prone. I am persuaded that this intoxication
> is the greatest danger of our time and that any philosophy which,
> however unintentionally, contributes to it is increasing the danger of
> vast social disorder.   (Russell, 2004, p. 737)

Russell is therefore extremely wary of philosophy which is no longer
moored to fact and is set free on a sea of belief and personal experience. He regarded it as a door to disorder. In fact this is precisely
what happened with the growth of the movement called existentialism in the mid twentieth century with the coming of the French
philosopher/writer Jean-Paul Sartre (1905–80) and the German
philosopher Martin Heidegger (1889–1976). Both sought personal
authenticity and the pursuit of freedom through angst. Inevitably this
quest for freedom meant choosing, often in anxiety, a course which
would lead to freedom but which nevertheless also affected the freedom of others. Bad faith (*mauvaise foi*) for Sartre was concealing this
basic moral freedom. This meant that values would be developed
responsibly but only in individual circumstances; unavoidably this
meant that ethics became more piecemeal, was developed responsibly but for particular situations. It was both a philosophy and an
ethical process that enabled greater individualism. Sartre's seminal
work *Being and Nothingness*, published in 1943, argues that the individual consciousness is a nothingness at the heart of being and must
choose for itself in the world, unaided by any norm of revelation,
objective morality, reason or convention. It was a philosophy which
contained a strong moral imperative to promote freedom, but little
if any objective standard by which that freedom might be obtained.
It was only a relatively short step from this to postmodernism.

Postmodernism is notoriously difficult to define. It is partly seen
as a reaction to modernity. Modernity was a scientific, rational, pro-
gressive and technological world-view which saw reason and science

developing human potential into the future. However for existentialism, war, suffering and poverty in the world seemed to deny this sense of progress which modernism hoped to engender. Postmodernism is the antithesis of this: rather than providing overarching explanations for existence it denies any metanarrative at all. Rather than looking for a universal cure, it proclaims there are many; rather than validating particular experience or world-views it holds that each is creditable and credible. In fact it seems to suit the times, in which many cultures are coming together; in which there is a desire not to discriminate but to affirm and celebrate all kind of experiences with the mottos attached like 'if it feels right do it', and 'if it is true for you it is true'.

Thus experiences and beliefs have proliferated with transforming effects; for instance, the act of shopping has passed from being merely a purchase to being a defining story, given a deeper significance and capable of holding its own in this potpourri philosophy of postmodernism. So the thing purchased, and the act of purchase, have both a defining and a renewing effect on the purchasers who see themselves as entering a recognized micro story, a particular subculture that gives meaning and definition to their existence. The tag phrase '*Tesco ergo sum*' contains more than a grain of truth. In other words, identity comes partly with the purchase, and retail therapy takes place in the cathedrals of shopping malls where people like to go for their weekly experience of renewal. But the experience soon ends when the fancy wrapping comes off; the experience sought is purchase rather than simply satisfying a practical need. Shopping is no longer a means to an end – it is an end in itself.

So where does this shift in culture, underpinned as it is by a shift in philosophy from Dewey, to Sartre, to Lyotard (the French exponent of postmodernism), leave us? In the postmodern world the church is one 'outlet' among many. The experience it has to offer is one of many in the spiritual supermarket of modern life. Whereas previously the church could inhabit a general philosophic system which, although given over to reason since the seventeenth century, was broadly accepting of the notions of fact, truth and event which in turn lie at the basis of the gospel, now the church must validate itself, declare its message in a world more interested in its effect than its cause. No wonder, then, that where the currency of truth in the postmodern mind is debased, or at least altered, the church with its message of 'the way, the truth and the life' finds itself in exciting new territory. The old philosophic systems with which it cosily cohabited for nearly fifteen hundred years being now in exile, and the new ones opening the door to 'vast social disorder', the church finds itself ill at ease or in a kind of exile itself. But in the new age the dis-order is the very thing that is celebrated, and the challenge now is to show that the experience of a genuine encounter with God allows for the reassembling of the metanarrative, proves to be both the most excit-ing explanation of life and the experience that puts all others in the shade.

A further reason for a sense of the exile in the church is that the Christendom construct has come tumbling down, and its legacy is in many ways all but passing. This was strikingly emphasized when on the same day as the Queen and Prince Philip celebrated their diamond wedding anniversary in Westminster Abbey, the House of Lords were debating whether lesbians had a right to artificial in-semination, parenting without any desire for a father. Two worlds coincided – which one was passing?

The end of Christendom

The end of Christendom has been widely charted by many authors and thinkers (not least the Paternoster series 'After Christendom': e.g. *Post-Christendom* and *Church after Christendom*, by Stuart Murray and *Faith and Politics after Christendom*, by Jonathan Bartley. Its demise has been evident to any casual observer over the past forty years and it is continuing to disintegrate.

Christendom as we shall see, especially in the next chapter, was a construct which occurred literally when Constantine appeared to abandon classical paganism for Christianity the night before the battle of Milvian Bridge on 28 October AD 312, when he took power in the Western Roman Empire. Following a dream, recorded by early church historians Eusebius and Lactantius, Constantine ordered his troops to put the Chi-Rho (the first two letters of Christ's name) sign on their shields. After victory in this battle, Constantine made the Christian faith the religion of the Roman Empire, started an exten-sive church-building programme and put bishops in positions of civic power. Christendom was born: a relationship between church and state, which was to exist, sometimes uneasily, until the middle of the twentieth century in Europe. But Christendom was not only an institution, but also a frame of mind from which people derived their identity and their place in society as well as a framework of service and obligations. Christendom in this sense reached its high-water mark in medieval Europe but persisted long afterwards (see Brown, 2001, pp. 1ff). In the next chapter we shall chart the waxing and waning of Christendom itself. The object here is simply to show Christendom's sudden disintegration as another cause for the church to perceive itself to be in a kind of exile. Later on we shall consider what a post-Christendom church might look like.

When I stepped out of 10 Downing Street in September 2007, having seen a Crown Patronage secretary responsible for Crown or Lord Chancellor's Livings, I instinctively knew that it might be the last time I would have the interesting and curious experience of entering the home of British executive power. It was an anachronism, an anomaly, a privileged legacy from the long years of Christendom in Britain and more particularly England. Earlier that year, soon after taking office, the Prime Minister, Gordon Brown, had said he wanted to reduce the patronage system and that as Prime Minister he would no longer be involved in choosing and presenting two names to the Queen for senior appointments in the Church of England. Not only that, but he appeared to raise the issue as to why Crown patronage officials, seeking to make appointments for cathedrals, canonries and parishes, should be funded by the state and housed at 10 Downing Street. It seems now that only a stock of notepaper will be needed for the Prime Minister to send a letter of appointment on behalf of the Monarch to the cleric chosen exclusively by the church – nothing else will be required. Although this is much welcomed by broad sections of the Church of England as a move to greater independence from the state, it is nonetheless a further weakening of the link between the established church and the state, which looks likely to continue. The removal of the Prime Minister from any participative involvement in patronage (although there is discussion about an adviser for the Crown being retained) is a symbolic moment, a further distancing of state from church, much longed for by many in the church but also rued by others.

However, the end of Christendom is not simply the breaking off of institutional relationships between church and state, and, because of our national history, one particular church at that. It is quite possible that the relationship will further alter with the probable decline of the numbers of bishops in a more elected Upper House in a further reformed House of Lords. The end of Christendom is also the end of a mindset in which there is a more than discernible shift of the church from the centre to the margins, from being so to speak 'on the board' to being a stakeholder, from being settlers to being sojourners or exiles, from being granted privileges to having fewer privileges than before in a pluralistic faith setting, from being able to control others to being vulnerable in our witness, from having a maintenance mentality to having a missional mentality, and from being an institution to becoming a movement (Murray, 2004, p. 20). The change of mindset comes about partly through the relentless challenge to the previously widely accepted beliefs and moral values of Christianity itself. The advocacy of those moral values or Christian precepts is now more often resisted by a secular society predicated on a postmodern basis.

We have reached a place where sincerely, but not uniformly, held views in the church, about (say) sexuality, are in collision with a state that is seeking to impose its view of human rights on all its citizens. This clearly emerged in the clash between government-funded Roman Catholic adoption agencies and the Labour Government, when the adoption agencies refused on the grounds of conscience to place children with gay parents in compliance with the terms of the Equality Act 2007, which outlaws discrimination in the provision of goods, facilities and services on the basis of sexual orientation. Despite a plea by Cardinal Archbishop Cormac Murphy-O'Connor to allow the agencies to continue their work without placing children with gay couples the government refused. The point is that although it is completely legitimate for Parliament to pass legislation in tune with the wishes of the people as agreed by their representatives (MPs), however much churches may disagree with some provisions, in this case a conscientious objection representing Catholic practice for two millennia was not allowed. The conscientious position of a well-respected religious minority was overruled by the secular will of the majority. So what we see is the insistence of the rights of people, offering with good intention a relatively new social experiment (the bringing up of children by gay parents) that overturns the practice of generations. Of course the age of a practice does not guarantee its rightness, but nevertheless it is founded on sincerely held beliefs and values. The clash in this case between church and state and the church's enforced submission to the will of the state is indicative of its movement into exile. (And the fear of many churches is that if they are not in future given rights to conscientious objection on similar issues, relating for instance to employment of practising gay people, then they may well find themselves unable to keep the law.)

Of course there is a wider and more complex issue here about whether religious scruples should be allowed in law; and if any religious convictions are to be accommodated in law, which should be admissible and which not. It seems that in the legislative tradition of this country greater accommodation is given in law to Judeo-Christian ethics as representing the majority view of the population, but inroads into this underlying religious perspective have been made by more secular definitions of human rights in the past forty years. For instance, the right of a woman to end her pregnancy with the agreement of two doctors is a classic example of a more secular view holding sway. The debate in February 2008 on whether any aspects of Sharia law can be accommodated within British law has also raised this issue sharply. The resounding answer has been that all citizens should be subject to the law of Parliament. Parliament is at liberty to make concessions to religious communities on a case-by-case basis, so that (for instance) the Muslim community has been allowed to make its own mortgage arrangements without paying stamp duty twice over, and churches have been given concessions with regard to employment law relating to issues of sexuality. What is clear is that there is a greater challenge to traditional Christian values by a more secular consensus and this too has been a sign of the passing of Christendom.

But the increasing distancing between Christianity and the culture and public bodies is not about sexual issues alone. Two university Christian Unions at Birmingham and Exeter have been prevented from meeting in university buildings by their Students' Union or guild because it was maintained that their leadership was not open to all, or that their stance on gay sex infringed human rights. On 26 November 2006 seven bishops and one retired archbishop wrote to *The Times* in support of the Christian Union's entitlement to meet in university buildings, at Exeter. A court case arising from this dispute has in fact found in favour of the Christian Union. Both the BBC and British Airways have in the past tried to prevent employees, a newsreader and a stewardess, from wearing a religious symbol, which in each case meant a small cross. Most borough or city coun-cils now only say 'Seasons Greetings' rather than 'Happy Christmas' in their Christmas cards for fear of giving offence, or a desire to distance themselves from being thought to subscribe to a particular religious position.

The point is not that the church wants Christendom revived, for it had its very large share of failures, including, for example, the en-dorsement of slavery (and did Jesus have in mind the founding of Christendom anyhow?), but to note here that even the legacy of Christendom is in the process of ending, apart from the stone and mortar of its extraordinary built heritage of churches, cathedrals and abbeys which continue to attract large numbers especially at Christmas. On the one hand we can rejoice at the beginning of the end of corruption, violence, arrogance and compulsion which char-acterized so much of Christendom in the past, but on the other hand we must see the gap which is opening up ever more between our cul-ture, the state and the church and the sense of exile that is bringing. The last of the four factors which have created this estrangement is the sheer diminution in size of the church in Britain since the 1960s.

Church shrink

During the late 1940s and the first half of the 1950s church mem-bership experienced the greatest annual growth since the eighteenth century (Brown, 2001, p. 172). But from the peak of the late 1950s there was a decline in membership for the rest of the century. Callum Brown writes about 'the discursive death of pious feminin-ity destroying the evangelical narrative' or put more simply, the role of the woman in the average British household began to change: no longer was she both the keeper of the family's conscience and the guardian of their household religious experience, she herself became restless and uncertain. The lyrics of the Beatles' song, 'She's leaving home', showed that old ways no longer satisfied and new horizons were demanded by young women.

It is well known that since the 1960s church membership in Britain has declined. The number of Methodists was at 733,000 in 1960 and is down to about 300,000 in 2008. From 4 million Roman Catholics in the 1960s there are now about 875,000 who attend Mass weekly; and Roman Catholic figures would be much worse but for the large number of Polish Catholics which now swell their ranks. Likewise, Anglican numbers have declined from 1.5 million in 1980 to about 867,000 in 2005 (Brierley, 2006, p. 28).

In 2005 The English Church Census was taken by Christian Research, the mostly comprehensive review of church membership in recent years. Its findings were both sobering and a little encouraging. Broadly speaking there are 227 denominations which were identified in Britain by the survey and these could be divided into ten main categories: four institutional churches including Roman Catholic, Anglican, Orthodox and URC, and six non-institutional churches or Free Churches including Methodist, Baptist, Pentecostal, Independent Churches and Emerging Churches. Almost all of them are in decline albeit pulling out of the precipitate nosedive which had characterized the decline in previous decades.

In the Anglican Church, which is my own denomination, church membership accounts for 1.7 per cent of the total population. The four institutional churches together account for 3.7 per cent of the population (Brierley, 2006, p. 24). Between 1979 and 1989 Anglican numbers dropped at the rate of about 40,000 a year, but between 1998 and 2005 the decline itself has reduced to 20,000 a year. Nevertheless among all the churches 34 per cent are growing. However, if this rate of decline continues in England church membership is predicted to be about 500,000 (Brierley, 2006, p. 28) in 2015. There is also a demographic time bomb in the figures as a large number of worshippers in the older institutional churches are over the age of 55. So the encouraging note, for instance, is that the Church of England is not declining as rapidly as it had been.

Pentecostal churches, thanks to the large element of Black Afro-Caribbean membership, have grown overall from 228,000 in 1979 to 287,000 in 2005 (Brierley, 2006, p. 33). But again independent churches taken as a whole including Free Independent Evangelical Churches (FIEC) and Brethren have declined from 235,000 in 1979 to 190,500 in 2005; and yet it is right to say that some of these churches have started to grow again since 1998, e.g. the FIEC. After the sharp declines in the 1960s, 1970s and 1980s, since the mid 1990s the rate of decline has slowed, and some church groups have started to grow; the greatest decline is seen in the institutional churches and the Methodist Church, and the most marked growth has been in black Pentecostal churches especially in London.

Indeed there are hot spots around the country. Around 20 per cent of all Christians to be found in England are in London. Black Pentecostal churches have increased by 68 per cent in London, with membership of 153,000. The largest single church, Kingsway International Christian Centre, is led by the Nigerian Pastor Matthew Ashimolowo, and presently has a membership of around 10,000 people. Other large churches include Hillsong, meeting at the Dominion Theatre and numbering 5,000, Kensington Temple, and high-profile Anglican churches in the capital such as Holy Trinity Brompton and All Souls' Langham Place with congregations in the thousands (Brierley, 2006, p. 45). Fresh Expression, a Methodist/Anglican movement in starting new expressions of church, has about 200 congregations or communities around the country accounting for some 17,000 members (see Brierley, 2006, p. 36, Table 2.14). Although a very hopeful new beginning has been made in the past seven years, Fresh Expression churches are not yet able to offset the overall loss of membership of 80,000 a year across the churches in England.

The main conclusions from this survey of church shrink since 1979 is that the institutional churches continue to decline at an alarming rate even if it is, as in the Anglican Church, half the rate of decline of before 1998. Some new churches, Fresh Expressions and ethnic churches are growing fast, some smaller independent churches such as the Vineyard Church and New Frontiers by as much as 70 per cent; but the rate of increase in a comparatively small number of churches will not, even at their encouraging rate of expansion, offset the large haemorrhaging in the institutional churches. If it were not for the black and ethnic churches then the figures would be far worse. We may soon be in a situation where the numbers in the institutional churches are similar to the numbers of Muslims and Hindus. The total church membership in England is 3.1 million with a further projected loss on current trends by 2015 of 19 per cent (Brierley, 2006, p. 24, Table 2.2). As such the church could be described as a remnant, some of it inhabiting ancient buildings redolent of a different age; a community trying to sing the Lord's song in a strange land, and being taught the tune by people who have come from overseas to give hope to an indigenous church in danger of being overwhelmed.

In this chapter we have charted those movements in post-war Britain which have substantially and irrevocably changed the religious landscape. A new pluralist society has arisen as a consequence of empire. The government of the country has, by and large, become secular (with a few exceptions like the provision for an act of worship at schools, which should be Christian) although at the same time religion has made a comeback with the New Age movement, Eastern religions and a widespread search for the numinous. The culture itself has changed markedly in many ways; and within an overall culture there are numerous subcultures, each with its own significance. The overarching understanding of life to which the majority once subscribed has broken down into a kaleidoscope of pieces; significance and validity being given to them by postmodern culture which looks to no single metanarrative of explanation. Christendom has been all but broken down and its legacy is being discarded. And in the midst of it all the churches have shrunk dramatically, although the shrinkage is worst in the institutional English church, not in the non-institutional ethnic church centred on nationalities that have entered this country in the past sixty years. So although the Christian situation of our time is more than a cause for concern, is it one for panic? Assuredly not. Why? Because although we are facing circumstances and a situation which is unparalleled in all our Christian history in England for the past fifteen hundred years, Christians know that the gospel remains God's answer to human need, it remains 'the power of God for salvation' (Romans 1.16) and despite all the church's many failings, for which we need to repent, God still remains on the side of his beleaguered church. And we know that God is ceaselessly working outside the church to achieve his purposes. But as well as all that, if we are in a kind of exile presently, then, as we have already seen with regard to Judah's sojourn in Babylon in the sixth and fifth centuries BC, it is there that God renews, teaches and reforms his people for the future. And so before looking forward to the kind of church we might be for this new age, we shall look back over the successive paradigms of church history to see how those in exile were often those who brought that renewal and change into being and responded to the demands of their times.

3

The changing paradigms of church history

Hans Küng in his magnum opus *Christianity: The Religious Situation of Our Time* recounts five paradigm shifts in church history before we reach our own time, which we have briefly looked at in the previous chapter. A paradigm revolves around and is produced by a set of religious and intellectual convictions and assumptions about the world and our place in it which gives shape to a resulting culture, obligations and institutions. We shall look very briefly at each of the five paradigms that Küng and others have traced in the West before seeing how often exiles at each stage were principally responsible for shifting the paradigm and so re-forming and renewing the church in its call to mission. The reason for looking back over the past is to understand that it is in part through this exilic process that renewal of mission in the church has come about; and that it should not therefore be too unexpected that, if the church is to be ready for the new world or paradigm which it entered after the 1960s, it too may experience a kind of exile now. Not only that, but through these changing paradigms of church history many individuals or groups, whose lives we shall consider in the next two chapters, experienced exile in various ways in the cause of renewing and reforming the church in its life and teaching.

The early Christian apocalyptic paradigm

We have already noticed that during the years of the Apostles and in the following two centuries until the coming of Constantine, the church faced persecution. Jesus himself suffered in this way and predicted that his followers would suffer similarly, for 'a servant is not above his master' (John 15.20) in this respect as in others. The Apostles Peter and Paul were most probably executed during the purges which occurred before the great fire in Rome in AD 64. But whereas Gallio, the Proconsul of Achaia, the brother of the philosopher Seneca (Nero's initial tutor) is reported to have said in reference to Christianity appearing in Corinth that 'he cared nothing for these things' (i.e. that he did not want to be bothered by them (Acts 18.17) and so threw out a complaint by the Jews against Paul in Corinth), a later governor of Bithynia, Pliny, took quite a different line.

Pliny was a quintessential Roman administrator, philosopher, philanthropist and writer of many letters to the Emperor Trajan (AD 98–117, one of the so-called five 'Good Emperors' according to Gibbon and Machiavelli) in which he asked, among many other things, how to handle the treatment of Christians. Trajan's advice was that although they were not to be hunted down, those who would not call on the gods, pray to an image of the Emperor and who would not offer incense or wine to the gods as a sacrifice or offering were to be executed (Lane Fox, 2005, pp. 566–7). So in the space of fifty years Gallio's lack of interest was succeeded by the political, scapegoating purges of Christians by the Emperor Nero, and later by the more settled policy of persecution of Christians as dangerous nonconformists by Pliny at the start of the second century AD. After all Christians would not go to the games, were generally pacifist and would take no part in the sacrifices at pagan temples, nor would they generally enter the Roman army in the years before Constantine. On the other hand they met in small groups, were well known for their care of widows, orphans and the poor, kept away from all pagan worship, sang songs, met in mixed groups of slaves and freedmen, numbered not a few prominent women among them, were followers of Jesus and waited for his return. They were certainly a different kind of people, and as the *Epistle to Diognetus* stated, 'they dwell in their own country but simply as sojourners' (i.e. exiles).

In the second century the church rapidly expanded but was also at times fiercely persecuted. Through the latter years of the second century and well into the third, Christianity spread vigorously through Syria, the Eastern Empire to Persia, North Africa, south-west France and Britain. In AD 314, three bishops from Britain attended the Council of Arles (H. Chadwick, 1993, p. 63). At the same time the Christian faith spread to both the middle and upper classes and became established in principal cities of the Empire like Carthage, Alexandria and Rome itself (Lane Fox, 1986, p. 272). The reason for its rapid expansion during the second century especially was its promise of fulfilment and contentment over against the Stoic philosophy espoused by leaders like the Emperor Marcus Aurelius, its demonstrable care of the poor and its promise of eternal life to a class of plebeians and slaves condemned to misery in this life. As Chadwick writes,

> The Christians found much that was congenial in Stoic ethics ('Seneca often speaks like a Christian' remarked Tertullian), and were not disposed to deny their indebtedness to its wisdom. The divergence lay in the Christian stress on the grace of God as making the Christian life possible, on the love of God (rather than individual self-respect) as the object towards which human striving should be directed, and on the outgoing activity of 'charity' towards one's fellow men.
>
> (H. Chadwick, 1993, p. 56)

The care of the poor was impressive. By 251 the resources of the church in Rome supported from a common purse 46 Presbyters, 7 deacons, 7 sub-deacons, 42 acolytes, 52 exorcists, numerous readers, door-keepers and a further 1500 widows and needy persons 'fed by the grace and kindness of the Lord' (H. Chadwick, 1993, pp. 57, 58). Not only that but Christian slave owners were encouraged to free their slaves in the presence of a bishop, and one ex-slave rose to be a bishop, notably Bishop Callistus in Rome (H. Chadwick, 1993, p. 60).

During the Apostolic period and later the church was beset with controversies, three of which stand out. The chief controversy which made its appearance towards the end of the first century was Gnosticism.

> The Gnostic heretics had appealed to the principles of Platonism to provide philosophical justification for their doctrine that the elect soul must be liberated from the evil inherent in the material realm to escape to its true home and to enjoy the beatific vision. Their deep pessimism about the created order was not quite fairly deduced from Plato, but there was sufficient plausibility about the argument to make it look impressive.
>
> (H. Chadwick, 1993, p. 75)

The results of this ragbag of speculation, theology and philosophy was to put in question the divinity of Jesus (since how could God assume what the Gnostics considered to be evil and corrupt human flesh?) and to give undue significance to an ascetic lifestyle which subordinated the flesh to the spirit, or conversely to a libertine lifestyle, since what is done in the body could not imprison the spirit of one who possessed *gnosis* (knowledge). At each of these points Gnosticism was a danger to the health of the church and it took the assembled firepower of Irenaeus, Clement of Alexandria and Justin Martyr to resist its blandishments.

Another attack on the church came through a prophetic individual called Mani in the mid third century who appeared in Persia and described our spiritual life as a constant battle between good and evil equally pitted against each other in which deliverance could come by following the teachings of Mani who could release good from particles of light to aid people in their struggle. The dualism of Manichaeism was its chief legacy and proved highly attractive to Augustine before his conversion (Lane Fox, 1986, pp. 561–71).

The last assault upon the church came from Montanism, a kind of highly charged form of Pentecostalism in which Montanus, a self-styled prophet, in about AD 166 with male helpers and two prophetesses emerged from Phrygia, North Africa, to call for radical purity, separation from the world and martyrdom, and claimed to speak directly on behalf of God (Lane Fox, 1986, pp. 404–10). For a time the brilliant apologist Tertullian was in their ranks, while Hippolytus of Rome criticized their excesses and called for a canon of Scripture by which all might be judged. For years the dispute rumbled on until Augustine of Hippo among others sanctioned force to bring them to heel (H. Chadwick, 1993, p. 91).

The second and third centuries AD saw persecution continue in the Roman provinces and this fuelled in those early years of the church the notion that all Christians were sojourners and exiles. Carthage, the Empire's second city, saw fierce persecution around AD 202 with the dramatic martyrdom of Perpetua who with her slave girl Felicitas were thrown to wild animals, at first naked, until the crowd objected that they should be fully clothed (Lane Fox, 1986, p. 420). Perpetua's diary, written while she awaited martyrdom, is as moving a document as any of its kind. In December 249 the new Emperor Decius issued an edict ordering sacrificing to the gods throughout the empire. Bishop Cyprian of Carthage went into hiding; the Bishops of Rome, Antioch and Jerusalem were martyred. New controversies emerged, and continued for centuries, about how those who had lapsed should be treated. Cyprian was eventually arrested and executed on

14 September 258. But a final and worse persecution broke out under the Eastern Emperor Diocletian's reign, precipitated by the 'failure' of an oracular sacrifice at Apollo's shrine at Miletus because Christians were present (H. Chadwick, 1993, p. 121).

In the Western Empire and in succession to his father Constantius, Constantine was proclaimed Emperor by the Roman soldiers in York on 25 July 306. All was soon to change; the exiles who typified the Apostolic church were to be given power in the state, and Christendom would begin to come into being. But before watching the building of the Roman paradigm we must move eastwards to Egypt, Syria, Palestine and Constantinople and see the building of a Hellenistic or Greek paradigm centred eventually at Constantinople, with which Rome would soon come to compete.

The Hellenistic or Greek paradigm

The educated world of the second and third centuries expressed itself in the Greek language, the New Testament was written entirely in Greek, and the defence of Christianity against Gnosticism and the dualism that came from the East as expressed in Manichaeism was mostly written in Greek. Greek, in short, was the educated language of the Greco-Roman world, only to be replaced gradually by Latin in the Western Empire in the fourth century. The founding of Constantinople by Constantine on 11 May 330 after his defeat of Licinius in 324 provided a new base for the development of the Hellenistic church (Küng, 1995, p. 197). It was only to be expected therefore that terms used both in the expression and definition of the Christian faith (e.g. the use of *logos* in John's prologue) and in its defence should come from Greek thought, Greek philosophers, and especially Plato. But Greek thought or intellectual terms also gave rise to speculation, and the history of the Greek-speaking church from the mid second century onwards was very much given over to a synthesis of biblical exegesis on the one hand and speculative thought arising from Platonic concepts on the other. This was especially true of the most influential Hellenistic theologian of the late second and third century, Origen. He was very much the mind behind the new Hellenistic paradigm which came to dominate in the Eastern Empire until the fall of Byzantium in the fifteenth century and which survived in the Greek and Slavic Orthodox churches.

Origen was a host of contradictions. His Father, Leonides, had been martyred when Origen was eighteen years old; this experience gave a steeliness to his work and manner which was a break with his more easygoing predecessor in Alexandria, Clement. Clement had written a more cheerful defence of Christianity employing the Platonic tradition against Gnosticism in the second century (H. Chadwick, 1993, p. 100). But although Origen inveighed against the classics, which he knew intimately, he nevertheless incorporated their concepts into his theology. He, like his contemporary Plotinus, the last great Greek Neoplatonist philosopher, had been taught by Ammonius Saccas. Origen held, like a good Platonist, that there was a pre-existent world before God's creation in which only one soul had not turned away from God 'and this soul was chosen to be united to the divine logos' (H. Chadwick, 1993, p. 105). He thus opened up a whole new area in Christology (the study of the person of Christ) in which Jesus' pre-existent status became as important as his earthly life and ministry. Again, few people ever studied Scripture as Origen did, with unending toil, loss of sleep and little food (H. Chadwick, 1993, p. 101) writing his *Hexapla*, a six-columned synopsis comparing four Greek texts of the Old Testament with the Hebrew text and a transliteration side by side. Nevertheless he employed a method of interpretation which looked for threefold meaning in the text, literal, moral and allegorical. In this method there was inbuilt tendency to look for the symbolic, metaphorical and spiritual or hidden meaning, which allowed for all kinds of exotic interpretations of Scripture.

The effect of this approach developed by Origen was to put a Hellenistic grid over the Scriptures in which it was necessary to describe the nature of Christ and the relationship of the three persons of the Trinity in Greek terms such as *hypostasis, ousia, physis, prosopon* and their Latin equivalents. When an excitable, attractive and populist preacher called Arius from Alexandria, in attempting to stress the monotheism of Christianity, denied that Jesus was of one substance with the Father, a battle of words began which was to divide Christendom for centuries. Athanasius, Arius' chief opponent in Alexandria, insisted that Father and Son were of the same substance (*homoousios*) and that the Son was not created and therefore was eternal. The Emperor Constantine summoned a church council at Nicaea in 325 where the word consubstantial (of the same substance) was agreed as describing the relationship of Father and Son. However, even Athanasius conceded that it was neither a perfect nor essential term in describing the relationship of Father and Son (Küng, 1995, p. 180). Nevertheless, what Athanasius had contended for and Nicaea had agreed, was necessary if the redemption in Jesus, as the eternal Son of God, was to be effective and people were to have assurance of forgiveness and eternal life. But the controversy rumbled on with different bishops seeking imperial backing for their stance on this issue. However, if one battlefield had been how to describe in Greek terms the relation of Father and Son, a further two doctrinal battlefields opened up: first the description of Father, Son and Spirit and their relationship to each other, i.e. the Trinity; and second, the relationship of the divine and human in Jesus. These two controversies were to further define as well as exhaust the Hellenistic church over the next two centuries.

In 381 the Emperor convened a Second Ecumenical Council of Constantinople, and after much toing and froing among Greek bishops with not a little animosity among them, the Nicene Creed was reiterated, but a conflict developed over how to describe the Trinity. Whereas in Nicaea stress had been laid on the one hypostasis of the Trinity, meaning the Trinity was *one entity in itself* (hypostasis), after the Council of Constantinople it became more common in the East to speak of three hypostases in which each person of the Trinity was an entity in themselves but in a common essence (*ousia* or *physis*). Seminal to the development of this trinitarian thinking which gave equal value to the Spirit were the Cappadocian Fathers who came from Asia Minor. They were Basil the Great, who after the death of Athanasius was the most prominent church leader in the East, Gregory of Nazianzus and Gregory of Nyssa. Combining the insights of Origen with the orthodoxy of Athanasius they were able to settle a new linguistic rule for describing the Trinity which was 'one in divine being, three persons or hypostases'. Once again the road to agreement was full of controversy – Sabellianism, which stressed the unity at the expense of the diversity of the Trinity, was rejected. Augustine in the West would further refine the doctrine of the Trinity in his *de Trinitate*, emphasizing that the Spirit proceeded from the Father and the Son. The imposition of the so-called double procession of the Spirit upon the Creed formed at Constantinople in 381 was to be the presenting cause of the split between the Western and Eastern

Church eventually. But the Trinity was not the only minefield for credal formulations: the nature of Christ was the other.

The Arian controversy had been about the nature of Christ: was he God or man? The resounding answer was that he was of the same substance as the Father. His divinity had been settled, theoretically at least, at Nicaea. Before Nicaea, the Gnostics had claimed that Jesus had only seemed to have come in the flesh (Docetism) and this view had been successfully disputed, chiefly by Irenaeus. After Nicaea, Apollinaris of Laodicea in Syria claimed that in Jesus the Logos replaced the human mind, thus compromising Jesus' humanity (H. Chadwick, 1993, p. 148). So now the task was on to describe, in Greek concepts and words, how the divine and human coexisted in Jesus. Two schools of theology with respect to this issue emerged: one from Antioch but taken up by Constantinople, the other from Alexandria. And not for the first or last time the resolution of Christian doctrine was caught up with the power struggles between cities and Patriarchates. Cyril of Alexandria cunningly and power-fully advocated a theology that stressed the singularity of Jesus' divine will at the expense of his humanity. This came to be called the Monophysite position, whereas the position in Constantinople advocated by Nestorius was of a firm distinction between Jesus' human and divine wills. The dispute sometimes led to violence: at the Council of Ephesus in 433 gangs of monks from Alexandria terrorized the proceedings (Küng, 1995, p. 191). Only with another intervention of the Emperor at the Council of Chalcedon (451) was a form of words hammered out in which the Council proclaimed that 'one and the same Christ exists in two natures unconfusedly, un-changeably, indivisibly, inseparably'. It was a form of words which should have satisfied both sides, but in fact the churches of Egypt (the Copts), Syria and Mesopotamia remained unreconciled to the point that the Muslims were later preferred by these 'Monophysite churches' to the hated Chalcedonian Greeks.

By the sixth century at one level the Eastern Greek Church centred on Constantinople was at the height of its influence. The Western Empire and Rome had fallen to the Goths in 410. The end of paganism had come. Justinian, who reigned from 527–67 and was a kind of second Alexander the Great, re-established the Empire in Italy, Egypt and Spain. He codified the law and built the great church Hagia Sophia in Constantinople. A new form of spirituality had arisen in the desert from the fourth century with first hermits, then monks and finally monasteries. The seeds of Christendom were very much apparent: the church was governed by the state; its controversies settled by the Emperor; its armed forces brought peoples subject to Christianity as in the Balkans; the priesthood became a separate class and the liturgy became their preserve. Jews were isolated and persecuted in the community. Religious art in the form of icons developed and with it controversy, with bouts of iconoclasm in the eighth century. But weakened by her many controversies, split into competing parts, more committed to ceremonial than compassionate action, the rulers in Constantinople, both ecclesiastical and civil, were quite unprepared for an event that took place on 11 January 630 when Muhammad rode into Mecca at the head of an army of 10,000 believers gathered in Medina. A hundred years later this at first martially deployed faith movement had overrun North Africa including Egypt, stretched as far East as Samarkand and the Indus and as far West as Spain. As Küng says, 'What did Islamic conquest represent for Christianity? Beyond question a catastrophe of world historical dimensions' (Küng, 1995, p. 342). Soon East and North Africa would be lost to the Muslims, and Byzantine Orthodoxy would spread North to the Southern Slavs, the Bulgars, the Romanians and Moravia until eventually it reached Kiev in the tenth century, and then on to Russia where it survived, despite two hundred years of Tartar rule. Orthodoxy moved North; Moscow became the new Constantinople after the latter's fall in 1453 to the Ottoman Turks, and both were united in their deep animosity to Rome from whom the Orthodox Church split in 1204. Only danger from the Turks gave some momentum to attempts to heal the split, but in the end these came to nothing. Rome had been building a new ecclesio-political paradigm and all were to be subject to its authority. We must now trace the history of the growth and development of this paradigm which came to dominate Western Europe.

The Roman Catholic paradigm

The growth of Roman Catholic supremacy in Western Europe was due to a number of factors. These were the establishment of a Roman orthodoxy which was substantially based on the works of Augustine of Hippo as well as that of the other three so-called Latin 'Doctors of the Church', Jerome and Ambrose (contemporaries of Augustine) and Pope Gregory the Great (540–604). The second factor was the development of the authority of the popes themselves, based on their claimed succession from Peter, who was called the 'rock' on which Christ would build the church (see Matthew 16.18). Third, Rome's power eventually grew as the Byzantine Church lost ground to the growth of Islam. The rapid development of Islam in Asia Minor and North Africa in the seventh and eighth centuries substantially diminished the influence of Constantinople and the Byzantine Church, while the destruction of Imperial Rome in 410 by the Goths, reducing it from a city of a million inhabitants to a mere 20,000, made the popes seek new alliances in Northern Europe with the Germanic tribes, and especially later with Charlemagne, King of the Franks. This eventually led to a kind of Roman Catholic hegemony in Western and Northern Europe.

Augustine, Ambrose and Jerome began in the fourth century to form a new orthodoxy, which was given shape by Augustine's writings and actions. His *de Trinitate*, as we have seen, gave equal value to the Spirit in trinitarian theology, stressing that the Spirit proceeded from the Father and Son. This became widely accepted in the Western Church and when in 1014 Pope Benedict VIII insisted on its inclusions in the creeds, so amending a previous Ecumenical Church, Council of the Eastern Church, it became the cause of the catastrophic split between Catholic and Orthodox churches. In addition Augustine opposed the so-called Donatist church leaders in North Africa. This controversy had been continuing for some eighty-five years and arose from the refusal by Bishop Donatus and many other church leaders to recognize the ministry and sacraments administered by lapsed priests or bishops ('lapsed' meaning that they had compromised their faith while under persecution). Augustine took the view that the sacraments were valid regardless of whether the exercising minister was 'pure', giving us the tenet so important in Catholicism that 'a sacrament is valid simply in dispensation' (Küng, 1995, p. 291). Furthermore, Augustine approved the use of force against the Donatists, permitting the confiscation of their goods and banishing them from their localities. In this way a further Catholic principle was laid down, namely 'the subordination of the individual to the church as an in-stitution which was the means of grace and salvation' (Küng, 1995, p. 290). Augustine further established the supremacy of

46

grace in salvation and the inability without it of people to work out their salvation by their own efforts. This was especially focused in the dispute with the British monk Pelagius who had emphasized the need for individuals, having received forgiveness, to gain salvation by their own efforts, a view which Augustine strongly resisted. Finally, Augustine made a powerful connection between original sin and sex, defining sex as the point of entrance for original sin, resulting in a view of sex and marriage in the Western Church which saw sex as a liability rather than a gift of God in the context of marriage. If these were some of the chief features of Augustinian thought, they were to be seminal in many of the stances of the Catholic Church as well as the quarry (besides Scripture) from which the Reformers would rediscover the theology of grace.

If Augustine's theology, together with the translation of the Bible into Latin (the Vulgate) by Jerome and the preaching of Ambrose of Milan, formed the body of Western and Roman Catholic theology, it went hand in hand with the development of the papacy as an institution. On 28 August 410 Rome fell to the army of Alaric, King of the West Goths, so occasioning Augustine's last great work *de civitate Dei* (on the City of God). For days on end the city was plundered, a civilization destroyed, the Dark Ages began, and in this chaos the popes saw an opportunity to form a new *imperium* on the ruins of the old one. Just as Rome herself was not built in a day, neither was this new ecclesiastical *imperium*, or rule. Already the Bishop of Rome, Damasus, building on precedents enacted by Bishop Stephen in the third century, appealed to the Petrine texts in the Bible to establish his authority further. After the fall of Rome popes made alliances where they could, initially with the East Goths and Langobards (Lombards) who were Arian Christians, having been originally evangelized by the Greek or Byzantine Church, and who made their centre of government at Ravenna. At the same time popes vigorously defended and extended their powers, sometimes through forgeries like the 'Donation of Constantine' which was a document purportedly based on a edict issued by the Emperor Constantine which said that the Bishop of Rome had been given civil rights and powers as well as the ownership of Rome and other lands and cities in Italy. But it was with the arrival of Gregory the Great in 590 that the shape of the medieval papacy was first fully laid down. Gregory was a bold administrator, leader and imposing pastor and able to popularize Catholicism by bringing it closer to the culture of the Germanic tribes through a generous use of legends which were impressive to his readers. At the same time he had formidable missionary zeal, initiating new missions to England under Augustine of Canterbury as well as to the West Goths in Spain. He thus substantially extended Roman Catholic influence. Wherever possible he had the sense to incorporate rather than alienate. At the same time Gregory had the wisdom to identify true spirituality, having been a monk who only reluctantly became pope. So he wrote the life of Benedict, whose rule was to become the yardstick of monastic life and Christian contemplative spirituality for centuries to come.

The years between the end of the sixth century and the emergence of the Frankish Kingdom on the Rhine in the eighth century under Charles Martel and Pepin were dominated by the rapid expansion of Islam. The conquests of the Umayyads (a Muslim Dynasty or Caliphate claiming common ancestry with Muhammad and based in Damascus, which saw Muslim rule extend West to North West Africa and Spain and East to Afghanistan during the seventh and eighth centuries) now took in all of North Africa, Spain and threatened both Sardinia and Sicily, close to Italy. During Pepin's reign a coalition of interests developed between the papacy and their dynasty. Pepin restored papal lands in Italy and his successor Charlemagne was crowned Emperor on Christmas Eve 800 by Pope Stephen in Rome. He was de facto the first Holy Roman Emperor. Christendom in the West had truly begun.

The Pope conferred legitimacy on the Frankish state and the Emperor's position; in return the Emperor provided political and military muscle, both in resisting Islam and further extending the empire through military conquest. Every year Charlemagne would take his barons on military campaigns; the defeated were given the option of captivity, execution or baptism. It's not surprising that Christendom grew! At the same time education gradually developed through Charlemagne's court. Augustine's writings were read at mealtimes in the court. And this programme of development was guided by his chief adviser, the Englishman Alcuin of York. A common liturgy including the Gregorian chant became prevalent in the Empire (see Küng, 1995, p. 358) and sexual abstinence and penance became familiar parts of German spirituality. But slowly, out of further chaos that followed the break-up of the Empire among

Charlemagne's heirs, the new world order, later known as the Middle Ages, was emerging.

The Middle Ages, which lasted from the tenth century until the Reformation, were in some respects unique. Richard Southern, the great Oxford medieval historian, was not exaggerating when he wrote, 'The history of the Western Church in the Middle Ages is the his-tory of the most elaborate and thoroughly integrated system of religious thought and practice the world has ever known' (Southern, 1970, p. 15). Arguably far greater integration was probably achieved in Europe then than now exists in the European Union. The papacy was the old Brussels. Canonical law emanating from Rome vied with national law in an endless tussle. The medieval world revolved around several great principles: the pre-eminence of the papacy in all religious matters; the exercise of kingship and feudal powers; the ministry of the monasteries and an all-pervading spiritual system and worldview which was common throughout Christendom and upheld by the church. No one was excepted in this system.

The growth of papal power occurred chiefly in the eleventh century. It was then that Roman ecclesiastical law was systematized by the Papal legate Humbert of Silva Candida. He determined that all bishops be appointed by the pope, overturning previous 'lay' appointments, especially in Germany by the Carolingian kings. It was he who precipitated the final break with the Eastern Orthodox Church over the insertion of the 'filioque clause' in the Creed in 1056. But more was to come. Later in the century the ever active and centralizing Archdeacon of Rome, Hildebrand, was elected Pope (as Gregory VII) even during the funeral rites of his predecessor. He now set about rigorously enforcing the powers of the papacy, insisting on mystical obedience, which meant that obedience to God equals obedience to the church, which in turn means obedience to the pope (Küng, 1995, p. 381). In 1075 he issued 'Dictatus Papae', 27 principles of papal primacy. A powerful illustration of this new-found power was the submission of the German King Henry IV to the Pope at Canossa. Having excommunicated and deposed Henry for continuing to appoint bishops as a 'layman', Henry arrived at the fortress at Canossa where Gregory was staying on 25 January 1077, barefoot and in traditional penitential garb (Küng, 1995, p. 386). After three days' penance in which the Pope had to be persuaded even to see this penitent king, the Pope lifted the ban of excommunication. The point had been well and truly made. But papal power and temporal kingship would always remain in uneasy relationship, with countless disputes with monarchs over the years.

Over the next two centuries papal power would wax and wane, reaching a high-water mark during the early thirteenth century before declining in the fourteenth century with the papacy at times divided between Rome and Avignon. Earlier popes had made common cause with the chivalric code of the medieval world to call a 'holy war', or crusade, against Islam. Pope Urban in 1095 preached the first crusade to reclaim the holy sites in Palestine to a hugely popular response of 'God wills it'. He then issued an indulgence, remitting punishment for sin for all who took part in the crusade. However what began as a war against Islam continued in later crusades as repression of any group who, like the Albigensians in Southern France, would not submit to the pope. The crusades, after initial but infamous 'success', did not succeed in their objectives and nor would spiritual movements in Western Europe which questioned the Roman Catholic paradigm easily be silenced by force alone.

Another great feature of the Middle Ages was the monasteries. The monastic movement in the West began under the leadership of Benedict. This movement of ascetic prayer, manual work and simplicity of lifestyle had originally begun in the Egyptian desert with individual hermits seeking greater holiness and separation from the world. Some were solitaries like Anthony whose life was written by Athanasius; others were organized into communities like the one by Pachomius at Tabennisi on the Nile. Other monks were more like spiritual vagrants and were censured by Benedict. New impetus to monasticism was given by the great insecurities that followed the invasion of Italy by the Goths in the fifth century. Commended by Gregory the Great, the Benedictine Rule quickly grew and spread through Northern Europe. From the eighth to the twelfth century Benedictine monasteries held sway. The monasteries prayed for the well-being of society, provided a way of satisfying the penitential stream in medieval society and a place where members of noble families, not suited to military adventures, could find a satisfying and respected vocation. But by 1100 the greatest days of the Order seemed to be over; some were corrupt, some had too few monks to survive, and monastic customs and duties had largely killed the inner spiritual search (Southern, 1970, p. 232). A new, more austere

Benedictine order had been founded in the twelfth century and the Cistercians, as they were called, fled to wild places where their more rigorous rule might be followed. At the same time Augustinian Canons began life in the towns, committed to a still simpler life (needing £3 a year to support a canon, as opposed to the more expensive £9 for a Benedictine monk (Southern, 1970, p. 246), they were committed to a gentler regime and to helping the poor. Both Cistercians and Augustinians flourished in their different habitats until the late fourteenth century, giving a new lease of life to the monastic movement. But it was the friars, who came into existence in the thirteenth century under Francis and Dominic, who were to catch the mood of their time. The origins of each would determine their future. The Dominicans were essentially a teaching order aimed at combating 'heresy', initially in Languedoc in France but reinforced by a rigorous commitment to an apostolic life. By 1221 when Dominic died their preaching and lifestyle were proving effective tools in the re-establishment of Catholic teaching especially in the universities. If the growth of the Dominicans was slow, the Franciscans grew like wildfire. If the Benedictines at best were characterized by obedience, the Cistercians by asceticism and devotion, the Augustinians to service, the Franciscans were characterized by poverty. When the 'little poor man' (*poverello*) Francis, met the most powerful man in the world, Pope Innocent III in 1209, a torch of spirituality was admitted into the church which swept across Europe. Its essence was commitment to poverty. By the early fourteenth century there would be about 1,400 houses with 28,000 friars (Southern, 1970, p. 285), a remarkable achievement in so short a time.

'The identification of the church with the whole of organised society is the fundamental feature which distinguishes the Middle Ages from earlier and later periods in history' (Southern, 1970, p. 16). Every child was baptized in the parish church (unless illegitimate), every person buried by the priest (unless a suicide), every village had a parish church, and since Theodore of Tarsus – an Asiatic Greek who became Archbishop of Canterbury in 668 – everyone in England would soon belong to a parish. The grip of the church on the medieval mind was pervasive; its teaching on purgatory, the sacraments, indulgences, penance, relics, veneration of Mary, military service especially in the crusades, together with the need for pilgrimage and masses for the dead, ensured that at every point of life and death the church took control. It was a paradigm of remarkable power which held in position the whole ecclesiastical edifice of clergy, monk and prelate. And supporting it was the whole cathedral-like structure of deductive rational thought built up by Thomas Aquinas (1225–74) who integrated the principles of Greek Aristotelian philosophy with Catholic theology in response to the rise of philosophy and biology in the universities under Albert the Great (Küng, 1995, p. 416). The resulting synthesis of reason and revelation was both influential and determinative in Catholicism. As Thomas supported the primacy of the papacy his work did not constitute a new theological paradigm (see Küng, 1995, pp. 416–30). So despite this extraordinary all-encompassing paradigm, which lasted around ten centuries, its very strength proved its undoing, with increasing abuse of authority, until its foundations were questioned at source by a brilliant, conscientious, tempestuous and courageous Augustinian friar who challenged the whole system single-handedly. His name was Martin Luther.

The Reformation

The shift in paradigm from medieval Roman Catholicism to a new Reformation paradigm began in the early fifteenth century. By the fourteenth century the integrity of the papacy had been greatly weakened. The power of the popes had been faced down by the growing confidence of kings and nation states. Philip, King of France, had captured Pope Boniface VIII in 1303 and imprisoned him; while Dante in *The Divine Comedy* banished this pope to hell and denied his right to rule spiritually or temporally. For a period in the fourteenth century the papacy was split between Rome and Avignon. And in 1378 two popes excommunicated each other. One of them, Urban VI, the most incompetent and disturbed of them all, executed five of his cardinals and tortured a further six.

By 1415 cracks were showing in the whole system but it was still a further hundred years until the nailing of Martin Luther's 95 Theses, challenging practices of Roman Catholicism, to the castle church door in Wittenberg. In 1415 the Council of Constance met. It attempted to revive the authority of the Council over the papacy, but soon after it popes reasserted their claim to supremacy. The Council heard the news of Henry V's impending invasion of France in pursuit of his claim on the French throne and shamefully it allowed Jan Hus, a Bohemian pastor from Prague, safe passage to the Council but then condemned him to death by burning for heresy. There were the stirrings of reform both in Holland and in England, with the Lollards and John Wycliffe. In the middle of the century the Turkish threat was rekindled and on 29 May 1453 Constantinople was taken, and the last Byzantine ruler killed.

The fall of Constantinople had massive repercussions for Western and Eastern Europe with which we still live today. A few years earlier in 1439 with the Turkish threat to the city growing, there had been a slight rapprochement between Eastern and Western churches over the wording of the doctrine of the Trinity at the Council of Florence. The agreement at this Council over the double procession of the Spirit was more expedient than heartfelt on the Orthodox side, and made in the hope of support from Western Europe in resisting the Turks. This was never forthcoming (Southern, 1970, p. 88). Fourteen years later Constantinople fell to the Turks. Orthodoxy moved north to Moscow, itself emerging from two centuries of Mongol and Tartar domination and now governed by Ivan III who took the title of Tsar of All the Russias, cementing his association with Orthodoxy by marrying Sophia, the niece of the last Byzantine Emperor. It was his son Ivan the Terrible who combined a rule of Mongolian cruelty and Russian obduracy that was unsurpassed in tyrannical character until the advent of Stalin. If Orthodoxy was now strongest in the North in Moscow, much classical learning previously held in Constantinople was scattered like spores to the West, not least to Florence, inspiring the Quattrocento Renaissance of classical learning and art, which first flourished in early Medici Florence and then later in Holland, Northern Germany and England. The return to classical sources, not least to the Greek language, and the coincidence of the first printing press created the intellectual and technological conditions for the Reformation.

By the early fifteenth century conditions for the Reformation were ripe. Papal authority, so centralized by the Borgia and Medici popes, was set to be challenged on the grounds of its abuse of power, both spiritual and temporal. In 1498 Savonarola, a Dominican friar of unusual asceticism who is famed for his 'Bonfire of the Vanities' in Florence, was excommunicated and later burnt for challenging clerical abuses. Sixteen years later Martin Luther, an Augustinian friar and

professor of theology challenged the whole edifice of Roman Catholicism and in particular the absolutist centralism of the Roman Curia,
its falsely based financial system, the system of indulgences (whereby time off from purgatory could be paid for by relatives buying
indulgences on earth), its neglect of the Bible and its misunderstanding of grace and the sacraments. The great fundamental question for
Luther was how a person is justified by God. His resounding answer
was 'by grace through faith'. The slogans of the Reformation were
'*solus Christus*', '*sola gratia*', '*sola fide*', '*simul iustus et peccator*' and '*sola
scriptura*' (Christ alone, grace alone, by faith alone, at once both justified
and sinful, Scripture alone).

> Luther's personal impetus towards reformation and his tremendous
> historical explosive effect derived from the same source: a return of
> the church to the gospel of Jesus Christ as it was experienced in a
> living way in Holy Scripture and especially in Paul.
>
> (Küng, 1995, p. 536)

A new paradigm had been created and because Luther was excommunicated by the Roman Catholic Church and because this teaching could not exist in the world of that time without civil power
(because the Pope had an alliance with the Holy Roman Emperor
who at that time was Charles V, the ruler of the world's superpower,
Spain), it needed civil power to both protect and uphold it. So for
the next 140 years there was a realignment in Europe between civil
powers with one or other of these paradigms: Roman Catholicism
or Protestantism. This was done with appalling loss of life.

By and large Northern Europe became Protestant and Southern
Europe remained Roman Catholic. This 'Reformation' as it became
known, coincided in England with Henry VIII's desire for a divorce
and this increased his willingness to break with Rome and establish
a national Protestant church. Holland fought Spain to establish both
its independence and Protestant self-rule. City states in Switzerland
embraced a variety of forms of Protestantism, notably Calvinism in
Geneva. Scotland welcomed Calvinism in the person of John Knox.
Northern German princes, with the support of Sweden, held off
the military assault of the Roman Emperor until the Peace of Westphalia in 1648. England under Cromwell and the regicides executed
its king, Charles I, to remain Protestant and to curtail absolute mon-
archical power, establishing a constitutional monarchy which came

to final fruition in the Glorious Revolution of 1688. France, having suffered lengthy religious wars, remained Catholic but accommodated the Huguenots in the Edict of Nantes in 1598 until its repeal in 1685, which precipitated a great stream of immigrants to London. Southern Europe for the most part remained Catholic.

The principles of this new Reformation paradigm, which was in time to find fullest expression in North America, were freedom to follow individual conscience and faith founded on personal experience rather than submission to the church; freedom to arrange the church in a way which was closer to primitive Christianity; and freedom to return to the original source, the Bible. These changes also affected the Roman Catholic Church inspiring the Counter-Reformation, which purged excess and abuse and precipitated a renewal of Catholic dogma, spirituality and liturgy in which the Bible became more central and the laity more prominent. But toleration was still a long time coming and deviants from Protestant orthodoxy were harshly treated (for instance Michael Servetus in Geneva was burnt for his non-trinitarian polemic in 1553). New movements within Protestantism grew, for instance pietism, which flourished in Northern Germany and spread to England and North America in the form of Puritanism; pacifism in the Mennonite Church and individualism in more extreme Baptist movements like the Anabaptists. But with this permission for the individual to explore and enquire came the seeds of the final paradigm shift which would take place in the seventeenth century and bring in the period of Enlightenment.

The Enlightenment or modern paradigm

The events of the sixteenth and seventeenth centuries paved the way for a radical reorientation. The Turks had been held at Vienna in 1529 by Charles V, and eastern borders were now more or less secure. The age of discovery led by Columbus opened up a new world and a new world-view. At first South America was used as a source of gold and silver for Spain as well as a new arena for military mission for the Catholic Church led by the Conquistadors. Later missionary work by the Jesuits was of a different order. The religious wars of the late sixteenth and seventeenth centuries exhausted European nations and slowly a new politico-religious map took shape. Gradually the age-old medieval battles between popes and national rulers were replaced by a struggle for hegemony among European nation states which was to continue unabated in Europe and overseas until 1945 or even 1989 (the fall of the Berlin Wall). Spain was eclipsed by the mid seventeenth century by France under Louis XIV, who became dominant on the continent of Europe until 1720. Versailles was the emblem of the age, symbolizing Louis XIV's dictum, *'L'état, c'est moi'.* Built by 30,000 labourers, the palace was 'the cult palace for the absolutist monarchy and its paraliturgy' (Küng, 1995, p. 655). By contrast England's earlier revolution prepared the way for a Protestant nation led by a constitutional monarchy with strong trad-ing and commercial instincts.

In this new post-Reformation age intellectual and above all scientific inquiry grew. The distinctive difference between the seventeenth century and all its predecessors was the scientific progress made. Galileo (1564–1642), one of the great founders of modern science, was born on the day Michelangelo died, and Galileo died on the day Newton, his great successor, was born (Russell, 2004, p. 489). The two of them are the fathers of modern science, drawing their conclusions from observation and empirical data and no longer from a combination of revelation and reason as found in Aquinas. For the first time their discoveries, along with those of Copernicus and Kepler, moved science well beyond the understanding of classical times. The earth was dethroned from pre-eminence, a heliocentric system was proved, distances between planets were measured, the orbiting of the sun by earth was understood, the force of gravity discovered, principles about electricity and light made clear. A world system was revealed through scientific observation, leading to new world-views and a new metaphysical awareness which broke open the medieval world. The Catholic Church sought to impugn Galileo, hauling him before the Inquisition in 1632 and putting him under indefinite house arrest. But the truth could not be arrested nor the progress of science prevented.

At the same time Descartes became the most important of the Enlightenment philosophers (1596–1650). Leaving France for Holland and then Sweden, he began a process of enquiry free of all previous method which might give both mathematical and philosophical certainty. Assuming the mind to be a *tabula rosa*, or blank sheet, doubt or scepticism could be the tools by which things might be tested: 'As long as I am doubting I am thinking and as long

as I am thinking I am' (*cogito ergo sum*) (Küng, 1995, p. 671). Summoned by his patron Queen Christina of Sweden he would discuss
philosophy with her at five in the morning (Küng, 1995, p. 671). But
his work was mostly published posthumously for fear of persecution.
Newton's *Essay concerning human understanding* published in 1690
gave a systematic enquiry into human reason based on an empirical
method of proof which is apprehended by the senses, including
reason itself. Rationalism was truly of age and there followed a
school of empirical philosophy building on Descartes, Spinoza and
Leibniz which was chiefly British, led by Locke, Berkeley and Hume.

Soon these scientific and philosophic discoveries took on a more
political edge with a demand for change and nowhere more urgently
than in France, where absolutism had led to repression both of
ideas and of economic development, especially for the middle classes.
Rousseau and Voltaire gave voice politically to more revolutionary
ideas which took root in conditions ready for change. The violence
of the Revolution only proved the deep-seatedness of the malaise in
the *ancien régime* but also the bloodlust of the Paris mob. With the
French Revolution in 1789 an almost secular state was born, while
a few years earlier across the Atlantic another Revolution occurred
which, although as passionate about freedom, was not iconoclastic
about its recent past, nor did it need to be. While in France there was
widespread disenchantment about the role of the church in supporting the *ancien régime*, in the United States religious freedom was an
essential part of the new constitution. Secularism in Europe resulted
in part because of the institutional role Christianity had played in
conferring legitimacy on corrupt regimes during the long years of
Christendom.

This modern or Enlightenment paradigm continued through the
nineteenth century, although in Europe rationalism went through
a filter of Romanticism from the late eighteenth century. Kant
(1724–1804) the leading philosopher of the late eighteenth century,
explored more closely the relationship between the objective and
the subjective, the observed world around us and the limits of our
knowledge. He conceded that by reason alone we cannot grasp the
principles that govern the world: hence his famous saying, 'I have
found it necessary to deny *knowledge* in order to leave room for
faith'. He readmitted the need for faith, which was further explored
by Schleiermacher in Berlin. For much of the century the German

school of philosophy sought to reconcile scientific observation with the aspiration of the human spirit, while leaving open the probability of God. But as the century progressed the philosophies hardened with the arrival of Marx and Nietzsche. Building on the philosopher Hegel Marx suggested the way forward was through the dialectic of class struggle in which the people owned the means of production, bringing freedom and prosperity in its wake. Nietzsche, on the other hand, advocated a breed of supermen who would rule the world with iron discipline and will-power. Between them they laid the way for the emergence of communism and fascism which signalled the end of the modern world and ushered in the paradigm in which we now live. The fifth paradigm was ending and a new one has barely begun.

Through these two thousand years of history, divided into these five paradigms, we have charted, in the briefest possible way, the church and its mission. We have seen how it has failed, adapted, survived, suffered and thrived, sometimes all too briefly. As with so many human organizations, when it became powerful it became corrupt, despite claiming to show the grace and humility of God in Christ. For much of the last two millennia the church, in conjunction with rulers in Christendom, created paradigms of power which it later had to change or abandon, if it was to reflect in any way the Lord it claimed to serve. Often these essential changes were only brought about through exiles – individuals, groups or movements willing to go into different kinds of exile to bring about renewal of mission, or reformation of the ministry of the church. It is time to focus a little more clearly upon these exiles and to remember them and be inspired by their witness in preparing ourselves for what is quite possibly a new kind of exile today.

4

Exiles in the first millennium

In considering exiles in the first millennium of church history we are looking at a small selection of people well known for their leadership who are representative of a host of others. We have already seen how in the first thousand years after Christ there were three distinct paradigms of 'church': the apocalyptic paradigm of the Apostolic church; the Greek paradigm centred at Constantinople; and then the Latin Roman Catholic paradigm which was well established at Rome by the millennium. We will look at five people or movements who experienced exile in the cause of taking forward or renewing the mission of God in their day and whose example remains an inspiration for us today.

The Apostle Paul and the Apostolic era

Both Peter and Paul regarded themselves as sojourners or exiles in the world. They both had a sense of the Lord's imminent return: the time therefore was short, and the mission entrusted to them was urgent. In his second letter Peter thought he needed to give instruction as to why the Lord's return appeared to be delayed, when he wrote, 'The Lord is not slow in keeping his promise [his return], as some understand slowness. He is patient with you, not wanting anyone to perish, but everyone to come to repentance' (2 Peter 3.9). Likewise Paul awaited a Saviour from heaven who would end his exile here on earth and who 'by the power that enables him to bring everything under his control, will transform our lowly bodies so that they will be like his glorious body' (Philippians 3.20–21). In view of this great impending change which was the fulfilment of the Christian's hope and salvation, the consummation of all things, Paul recognized there was a provisionality about life on earth. Again, writing to the Philippians he readily talks about the possibility of his either departing to be with Christ, which is far better, or remaining 'for your progress and joy in the faith' (Philippians 1.25). However, he is convinced that he should remain, but at the same time he knows that his home is in heaven and therefore he is a temporary resident or exile on earth. Again, we find him ruminating about his existence on earth, putting his life in the same perspective in his correspondence with the Corinthians. While they exalted their wisdom, eloquence, prowess and gifts, Paul seems to sound a contrasting tone. He speaks of weakness, trembling, foolishness and hope. So he says, 'While we are in this tent [body], we groan and are burdened, because we do not wish to be unclothed but to be clothed with our heavenly dwelling, so that what is mortal may be swallowed up by life' (2 Corinthians 5.4; see the whole section 5.1–10). For Paul it is the groaning of an exile and the burden of ministry and mortality. And finally speaking of this exiled life taken up with mission, he says a little later that he and his fellow workers are 'known, yet regarded as unknown; dying, and yet we live on; beaten, and yet not killed; sorrowful, yet always rejoicing; poor, yet making many rich; having nothing, and yet possessing everything' (2 Corinthians 6.9–10). As he said in his first letter, 'Up to this moment we have become the scum of the earth, the refuse of the world' (1 Corinthians 4.13b).

In summary Paul, like his fellow Apostle Peter, saw the paradox of his ministry (having nothing, but making many rich) not only as being in step with Jesus who became poor that we might become rich (2 Corinthians 8.9) but also as stemming from the paradox of his existence: having a home in heaven but being exiled here on earth. As an exile he was a temporary resident with a permanent message; having an incomplete life and salvation now but nevertheless a firm hope of homecoming and the fulfilment of all his longings. And while he was an exile he must complete the course he had been set to run (see 2 Timothy 4.7). No one expressed better the tensions of exile in the Apostolic period than Paul, and he gave a vocabulary of exile which would cascade down the years of Christian history and experience.

Athanasius

One who knew Paul's way of life and teaching better than most was the fierce protagonist for the truth of the incarnation and the first advocate of the eremitic life, Athanasius. In 328, about two hundred and fifty years after Paul, Athanasius became the Bishop of Alexandria; located in present-day Egypt, Alexandria was considered the second or third most important city in the Roman world. Athanasius staunchly confronted the Arian heresy for 45 years. Arius, a presbyter from Alexandria, had questioned the divinity of Jesus, writing: 'The Son who is tempted, suffers, and dies, however exalted he may be, is not to be equal to the immutable Father beyond pain and death: if he is other than the Father, he is inferior' (H. Chadwick, 1993, p. 124). Arius made himself popular with the dock workers of Alexandria (the great grain port of the Roman world) by writing sea shanties, and was eagerly followed by cohorts of young women touched by his attractive manner and passionate and eloquent speech (H. Chadwick, 1993, p. 124). However, it soon became clear that the doctrine of Christ as human and divine was at risk and the Emperor Constantine called all the bishops to a council at Nicaea where the orthodox Nicene Creed was hammered out. But this was by no means, as we have seen, the end of Arianism and indeed the cause was taken up immediately by a scheming and politically effective bishop, Eusebius of Nicodemia, who had signed up to the Nicene Creed (but evidently took its words to mean what he wanted them to mean) and who sought to depose from their bishoprics the leading pro-Nicene bishops, among whom was Athanasius. Athanasius was a fierce defender of the Nicene faith, sometimes to the point of rashness, so that Eusebius was able to secure his dethronement for his harsh treatment of a group of Coptic Christians called the Melitians. When Eusebius persuaded the Emperor that Athanasius had threatened to halt the grain supply to Constantinople if he was not supported by the Emperor, Constantine agreed in a fit of anger to his dismissal and Athanasius was exiled to Trier in Gaul. His exile was not due to his orthodoxy but rather to the manipulation of his intemperance by an opponent at court.

After the death of the Emperor in 336 Athanasius was invited to return, but was hounded by the Eusebians for not getting the permission of a synod to resume his see, and he was consequently exiled again. Eventually he returned to Alexandria in 343, remaining there ten years with the support of the Western Emperor Constans. But when Constans died in 350 and the whole Empire was governed by the Arian Constantius, Athanasius' fate, as the chief protagonist of the anti-Arian party, was sealed. Constantius was persuaded by the Arians to adopt their position and imperial power was now used to gain the submission of the Western bishops to a more Arian position; the arrest of Athanasius was to follow. It was at this point in 356 that Athanasius fled Alexandria, escaping to join the ascetic movement in the Egyptian desert. There, concealed from the authorities by the devoted monks in Upper Egypt, Athanasius took to an eremitic way of life.

For six years he shared a monastic way of life. He wrote powerful pamphlets defending orthodoxy, not least *Against Pagans* and *On the Incarnation*. He espoused the spirituality of the desert, and wrote the classic life of the hermit Anthony. After the death of Constantius he was allowed back to his see but with the coming and going of emperors in swift succession, Athanasius was in and out of exile like a yo-yo. In 366 he was finally allowed to return and he died in post on 2 May 373.

As a character Athanasius was often fiery, occasionally violent in language, uncompromising on matters to do with faith but 'willing to overlook differences of language where the essential was agreed' (Thomson, 1971, p. xvii). So later in the Arian controversy when individual words were at the heart of the dispute and three positions had emerged, Athanasius was able to make a statesmanlike agreement. The three positions were as follows. First the radical Arian position was represented by the Antiochene school of theology led by a clever layman Aetius, supported by George of Alexandria and Eudoxius of Antioch, who said that Christ was part of the created order. Second, a middle position espoused the Greek word *homoiousios* which meant that the Son was *like* the Father, 'as a perfect image resembles its archetype' (H. Chadwick, 1993, p. 141). Third, the *homoousios* or Nicene party said that Father and Son were identical in substance. By 360, in the face of the ascendancy of Arianism at Constantinople, about which Jerome said 'the world groaned to find itself Arian', Athanasius made an important compact with the *homoiousios* party led by Basil of Ancyra, writing, 'Those who accept the Nicene creed but have doubts about the term *homoousios* must not be treated as enemies; we should discuss the matter with them as brothers with brothers; they mean the same as we, and dispute only about the word' (quoted in H. Chadwick, 1993, p. 144). It was this alliance, born out of trust between Basil and Athanasius, cemented by a common intention although expressed with different words, which forged an agreement that would finally prevail, albeit only 20 years later when the Emperor Theodosius was willing to enforce it.

In his final years Athanasius would be drawn into the defence of the Holy Spirit as fully part of the Godhead in his *Letters to Serapion* but by then he was regarded as the elder statesman of the church, the only surviving bishop who had been present at Nicaea, who had suffered in exile but remained firm, and whose alliance with Basil had created the possibility of a final triumph for the orthodoxy that Father and Son were equally God. His years of exile ensured both the truth of the gospel and a spirituality which emanated from the desert which would in turn profoundly influence the church in the West. His willingness to embrace exile repeatedly was vital for the defence of divinity of Christ. His staunchness was able to renew the church; his embracing of exile provided a model for others to follow.

John Chrysostom

Only 25 years after Athanasius' death a new Bishop of Constantinople – also no stranger to the desert – John Chrysostom, somewhat reluctantly took centre stage in the life of the church of the Eastern Empire. John was a brilliant, energetic preacher, known as the 'Golden Mouth', and implacably on the side of the poor. Schooled in the desert spirituality, he followed the ascetic tradition of Origen, Evagrius and Cassian. His support of these monks and his puritan lifestyle made him an uneasy member of the court in Constantinople, and an enemy of powerful voices like Epiphanius of Famagusta, Cypus, an early iconoclast.

Chrysostom's origin as a spiritual leader arose from the desert. The ascetic movement which took root in the desert in the Nile delta had begun early in the fourth century. What began as an individual quest for holiness as an ascetic or hermit's life, developed first into community (*coenobium*) and then under the influence of Basil of Caesarea in Asia Minor into a professed community. In Syria and Mesopotamia the ascetic life gave rise to more idiosyncratic devotion, not least that of Simeon the Stylite, and the other pillar dwellers. Simeon lived on top of a column giving wisdom to the crowds who came to him and was consulted by governments and individuals alike (H. Chadwick, 1993, pp. 180–2). But by AD 375 a dispute among these desert communities or ascetics had broken out, largely over their response to Origen. Epiphanius launched a broadside against Origenist theology, both his intellectual speculations and his symbolic interpretations of Scripture (which were many), as well as against the use of icons and pictures to decorate the walls of churches. A group of Origenist monks in Egypt called the Tall Brothers – presumably on account of their height – were expelled by Theophilus of Alexandria. They appealed to Chrysostom who took up their cause, so setting him against Theophilus, who became an implacable opponent.

John had abandoned a promising career in the civil service at Antioch in Syria to become a monk (*c.* 373). But in 381 he was made deacon, and served under Bishop Flavian of Antioch. In 386 he was made a presbyter, and soon became known as an able and eloquent preacher. He acquired a vast popular following in Antioch in 387 on account of his remarkable and radical preaching in which, among other things, he was prepared to criticize the Emperor's overbearing taxation policy. John was invariably on the side of the poor, led a spare and ascetic lifestyle himself and consistently criticized luxury wherever he found it. When made Patriarch of Constantinople in 397 he confronted two issues, the luxury of the Court and the controversy over Origen's teaching, which raged particularly in Alexandria and Egypt. He might have survived if he had taken on one of these, but to antagonize the Emperor's wife, Eudoxia, by his criticism of her extravagance and the Bishop of Alexandria for his (the Bishop's) hostility towards Origen was to place himself in an extremely vulnerable position. He continued his monkish ways in a sophisticated and metropolitan city which was seeking to become 'the New Rome', eating alone because of his weakened stomach, sacking corrupt clergy, and hardly espousing the building programmes of ambitious bishops who came seeking financial support in the capital.

In June 403 Theophilus, the Bishop of Alexandria, arrived at Constantinople summoning a Council at Chalcedon in the palace of the Oak on the South or Asian side of the Bosphorus. John did not attend, knowing their hostility towards him, and he was deposed. He also criticized Eudoxia for some shady property deals, making an implicit comparison between her and Jezebel. This did nothing to endear him to the Emperor and when he was deposed by the Council of the Oak the Emperor readily accepted their decision and John was sent into exile (H. Chadwick, 1993, pp. 184–91).

At first he was banished to a small village on the borders of Cilicia and Armenia; later he was further banished by the Empress to Pityus in the Caucasus. For three months he wearily trudged towards Pityus but he collapsed and died en route in the chapel of St Basiliscus on 14 September 407. Initially his memory was treated like an ecclesiastical football, embraced by some and vilified by others, until ironically, given the later split between the Roman and Byzantine Church, his legacy was taken up by Pope Innocent I in Rome while John was still condemned by successive Bishops of Alexandria and Constantinople. Nevertheless John's memory was cherished by the people who in turn refused to accept his successor, worshipping outside the city instead and not in the cathedral. Only some years later would John be remembered in the Eucharistic prayers or Diptychs in Alexandria and Constantinople. But in the end his influence was to be substantial; his sermons 'remain today the most readable and edifying of all discourses among those of the Church Fathers' (H. Chadwick, 1993, p. 186), his radical espousal of the poor was influential and his name was given to the chief liturgy of the Orthodox Church today. He was another outspoken exile whose life in the end proved highly influential. And the spirituality that formed him in the Syrian desert was conveyed through other Origenist monks, notably Evagrius and Cassian, to form the greatest of all Western monastic spiritual traditions, that of the Rule of Benedict.

Benedict

So far our exiles from the first four hundred years of Christian history have been mostly drawn from the Eastern or Greek-speaking Church, representing the Apostolic and Greek paradigm in the church's history. Paul, a Jew from Tarsus, was sent out by the church at Syrian Antioch although he ended his life in Rome. Athanasius, from Alexandria in Egypt, redoubtable theologian and exiled hermit, defended Nicene orthodoxy tenaciously throughout his long and eventful episcopate, dying towards the end of the fourth century. Chrysostom, drawn from the Syrian desert into arguably the most prestigious see in the Empire, was essentially more at home in the desert or in being free to preach passionately what was on his heart and in the Scriptures than in the metropolitan city of Constantinople with all its courtly intrigue. But from now on our focus moves to the Western Church based at Rome, and to a man who with consummate brevity and skill distilled the lessons from the East into a monastic rule for the Western Church, and then finally the focus shifts to the unique brand of Northern spirituality to be found in the Celtic Church.

Just years after John Chrysostom's death in the Caucasus, Rome fell to the Huns. Augustine in North Africa at Hippo observed Rome's fall and was inspired to write of the eternal city, the City of God; and by the time Rome was sacked a second time in the middle of the century the previous classical age was well and truly over and Christianity had to survive among the marauding hordes of Huns, Goths, Vandals and Lombards which swept through Italy. The way Christianity was in the first instance to survive these tumultuous times and later thrive was through the establishment of strong disciplined Christian communities or monasteries, and the most influential and enduring of these was centred on the teachings of Benedict of Nursia.

Benedict was born around AD 480.

> He built an ark to survive the rising storm, an ark not made with hands, into which by two and two human and eternal values might enter, to be kept until the water assuaged, an ark moreover which lasted not only for one troubled century but for fifteen, and which has still the capacity to bring many safely to land. (de Waal, 1999, p. 1)

Little is known about Benedict himself; his life and work are conveyed to us through Gregory the Great's second book, the *Dialogues*. Benedict was born in the Umbrian district of Nursia into a family of high station. He went to Rome to study the liberal arts which he then abandoned and as a layman spent two years at Affile and then Subiaco, 'where for three years he lived a solitary life in a cave on a hillside, a mountain fastness surrounded by scenery formidable in its wild beauty, with a view of the ruins of Nero's palace and the broken arches of a Roman aqueduct lying below, symbols of the crumbling imperial greatness' (de Waal, 1991, p. 2). However, Benedict was not left to himself and his solitary life, but was pressed by neighbouring monks into establishing 12 small monasteries in the area, and finally took a group of them south to Monte Cassino where in 528/9 he formed his first complete monastic community based around his famous, terse, simple and wise Rule.

The Rule itself was a synthesis and development of previous monastic traditions which most probably had come from the East and the desert tradition forged in Egypt, Palestine and Syria. Evagrius, a close friend of Gregory of Nazianzus, one of the Cappadocian Fathers, left Constantinople after an unrequited love affair for the Egyptian desert. There he became a leading light in the monastic movement, ordering both the contemplative life and the discipline of contemplation itself as well as listing the eight deadly sins adding *accidie* or weariness to the other seven (H. Chadwick, 1993, p. 181). Likewise Cassian, a protégé of Chrysostom who finally ended up in Marseille after John's fall and exile, wrote extensively about the external ordering of the monastic life (his *Institutes*) as well as its spiritual inward journey (the *Conferences*). These writings, together with Athanasius' *Life of Anthony*, may well have been available to Benedict. We do know that he based much of his own rule on another anonymous text called the *Rule of the Master*. However, the Rule of Benedict, the most influential of all monastic rules, and possibly the most important spiritual document outside the Bible itself for the next seven hundred years, was a fresh, flexible and formative document capable of inspiring Christian community both in the sixth century and in the twenty-first century (witness the recent television series *The Monastery*).

The Rule of Benedict is brief, not more than 12,000 words. It revolves around a threefold vow and three interlacing activities of worship or prayer, meditation on the Word and manual labour. The day was divided between these activities. The threefold vow was of obedience, stability and *conversatio morum* (a continual change of heart). As de Waal says,

> 'The Rule knows much about the continuing paradox that all of us need to be both in the market place and yet in the desert; that if we join in common worship yet we have also to be able to pray alone; that if commitment to stability is vital so also is openness to change. There is no evasion of the complexity of life, and yet the final paradox is that running the way to God appears modest and manageable while at the same time it is total. These are the demands of extreme simplicity which cost everything.'   (de Waal, 1999, p. 14)

The disciplines at the heart of the Rule are listening to God in Scripture, for 'Holy Scriptures cries aloud'; some four hours a day were to be spent in this *lectio divina*. Listening involves being attentive to the Word of God, 'as not only message but event and encounter' (de Waal, 1999, p. 26) and, especially for the youngest brothers, being attentive to the Abbot and the older brothers. Listening should result in obedience without grumbling either in word or gesture. This process of listening and obedience was to be discharged in a balanced environment of stability and change resulting from commitment and openness in which all material possessions were held in common. And finally everything was to be suffused with prayer, both the communal prayer which took place seven times a day, and in the monks' private devotions. In such a way disciplined Christian communities were formed of brothers who lived a kind of exilic life, set apart from the world, capable of providing continuity and stability in tempestuous times, and from which mission could be continually launched into their local areas. What Benedict expressed, building on the experiences of the Egyptian and Syrian desert, proved a solid bulwark and an effective springboard for the ministry of the church.

Celtic Christianity

Interestingly a similar pattern of mission came to exist in a wholly different area, namely in the Celtic regions of the post Roman Empire. With the withdrawal of Roman legions from Britain in AD 407 in the light of the impending threat to Rome from the great movement of peoples in Northern and Eastern Europe, Britain was returned to a patchwork of tribal loyalties and kingdoms. Soon after this withdrawal Bede tells us that invasions of Saxons, Jutes and Angles crossed from Germany to Southern England (*Historia Ecclesiastica* 1.15). Over the next three centuries kingdoms waxed and waned. North of the Humber, the kingdom of Northumberland grew in prominence, combining together, when strongest, two ruling families of the Bernicians and the Deirans (Stenton, 1967, p. 37). Elsewhere Mercia in the Midlands and the kingdoms of Kent, Wessex and East Anglia grew powerful. With Christianity still relatively frail and at most still only a thin covering over the heathen practices of the past, two evangelistic enterprises entered the country from the west and south, the Celtic missionaries originating from Ireland and the mission sent by Pope Gregory the Great in AD 597 led by Augustine, an Italian monk known to later history as Augustine of Canterbury. In many ways these two roots of British Christian spirituality and patterns of mission, from Ireland and Rome respectively, were to grow in tension from then until the present day. In some respects they both needed each other as long as the strengths of each movement of mission did not strangle the other; in the end the Roman model was largely to supplant the Celtic.

Just as in the deserts of Egypt, Mesopotamia and Palestine hermits were to seek out desert places for an eremitic or monastic life, so in Celtic Britain the age of the Celtic saints was accompanied and followed by a period of monastic mission. If in the desert in the fourth century you sought a rock or cave, as did the testy translator and hermit Jerome in Palestine, so in Britain it was a windswept island or piece of wild coastline that was the preferred piece of monastic real estate for establishing community and launching mission. So places like Skellig Michael off the coast of Kerry – a bare rock in the Atlantic with beehive cells for the monks – or Iona by Mull, or Lindisfarne off the Northumberland coast were the perfect setting for the ascetic evangelism of men like Columba, Aidan and Cuthbert. If monks in the deserts of Egypt needed to be acclimatized to the sand and heat, in Britain they needed to be at home with the wind and the sea, with salt spray, birds and fish, with travel by boat as much by land. These three men and their sea-borne missions originating from Ireland are the most representative of the Celtic missions which swept through the fringes of Britain in the sixth and seventh centuries.

Columba set up a community at Iona from where he evangelized the Picts from 563; and for the next century it was to be the base for the evangelization of northern England and in particular the kingdom of Northumberland. It was from Iona that Oswald, later king of Northumberland, while himself in exile, 'received Christianity from the monks of Iona, the chief of nearly all the monasteries of the northern Irish and of all the monasteries of the Picts' (Stenton, 1967, p. 118). When safely in power Oswald called for a bishop from Iona, and Aidan with a company of monks arrived in Northumberland, setting up their community at Lindisfarne. 'Aidan himself was an ascetic evangelist, utterly indifferent to the dignity of a bishop, but influencing men of all ranks by his humility and devotion . . . His achievement was due to the popular veneration in which he was held' (Stenton, 1967, pp. 118–19). He was succeeded by monk bishops of a similar Celtic tradition in Finan and then Colman but latterly the church in the North was divided on whether to follow the Roman or Celtic dating of Easter and other variant practices relating to penance and the monks tonsure (haircut). After an initial debate between the Romanizing Wilfrid of Ripon and Colman, Oswald sided with the powerful Wilfrid and the die was cast. Gradually Celtic monasticism in England would give way to Roman practice. Colman retired to Inishbofin, an island off the coast of County Mayo in Ireland, and the decision to side with Rome was later ratified at the Synod of Whitby in 664, which finally settled the question of the date of Easter observance. Celtic traditions were carried on for a further twenty years by Cuthbert of Lindisfarne but although in his lifestyle and spirituality he kept alive the traditions of the original Celtic mission, he encouraged his followers to join with the rest of the English church accepting the metropolitan authority of Canterbury (Stenton, 1967, p. 126). For the best part of two hundred years the evangelistic, spiritual and ascetic dynamism of Celtic Christianity kept the gospel alive in the land at a time when the mission from the south of the country sent from Rome made little progress. The enduring attraction of Celtic Christianity today is a tribute to its innate respect for both creation and redemption, a spirituality which is both earthbound and heaven-sent, which is adapted to locality and is rigorously simple in life-style as well as supernatural in expectation. The Celtic missionaries isolated on their island fastnesses chose as their symbol of the Holy Spirit the wild goose, rather than the more domestic dove: theirs was a wild gospel indeed (Morgan, 2004)!

However the traditions of Celtic Christianity were not lost. As we have seen, Theodore of Tarsus became the unlikely Greek Archbishop of Canterbury sent by Pope Vitalian. Theodore himself was a monk, a scholar and divine. He was sent to England as its new archbishop at the age of 66 in AD 668, taking exactly a year to reach Canterbury from Rome (Stenton, 1967, pp. 131–2). Perhaps a more unlikely appointment could not be imagined, but it was to prove highly effective. It was his spiritual and administrative genius which originated the parish system in England though not at first the developed structure of later times. Initially, three types of churches (communities) were provided for: the *head minster* or cathedral church; the *ordinary minster* – a church with royal or episcopal patronage; and the *field church* – a new provisional church for lands recently brought into cultivation (what might now be called a Fresh

Expression). Nor was this structure a wholly Roman idea. Indeed, Cuthbert had a vision of such a system of pastoral and spiritual care when he was staying in a *parrochia* called Osingadum belonging to the Abbess of Whitby (Stenton, 1967, p. 148). A blend between Celtic and Roman had begun. Likewise Celtic monasticism was to blend with the Benedictine Rule so that in Lindisfarne the Rule became accepted and elsewhere at the monastery of Nursling in Hampshire (Stenton, 1967, pp. 158–9). Such communities empowered missionaries, not least Willibrord and his younger contemporary Boniface, who went as highly effective evangelists to the Frisians and thereby forged an enduring link between the Frankish court of Charles Martel, his son Pepin and grandson Charlemagne with the English church and court in Mercia. Monastic communities later spilling into parish communities were the seedbed for the evangelization of the country. Although the Celtic forms of monastic life gave way to the more structured Rule of Benedict, the heavenly fire that had brought them into existence was the fire of Celtic missionary service so well adapted to both the landscape of Britain and the temper of the people.

As we look back over the theme of exile in the first millennium we can see it present in the Apostolic mind in the apocalyptic period in which there was clear expectation that Christ would return imminently. Exile was the lot of many who defended the truth of the incarnation especially in the years following Nicaea when Arianism was strong; no one illustrated this better than Athanasius himself. Exile was also the lot of those who got on the wrong side of powerful lobbies of particular theologies when they were supported in turn by the court or civic power, such was Chrysostom's fate. But with the fall of Rome and the beginning of the Dark Ages which were to last the best part of five hundred years (and as far as the classical arts and languages are concerned until the Renaissance itself), the gospel survived to a large extent by the formation of tight-knit communities which were nevertheless witnessing to the world. This was most powerfully expressed by two movements in the church, one originating from the ruins of Rome and the other from the wilds of windswept islands off Ireland, Scotland and Northumberland. They not only nursed and maintained the faith with their commitment to listening to the Spirit and the Word of God but acted as the wombs from which missions would be constantly generated. Popes and kings turned to them and local people trusted them. These exiles were the source of renewal and revival. The exiles of the second millennium were by contrast, and by and large, men and women who had to face kings and popes for the reformation of the church along the original lines of what their forebears had fought for, which now men and women of power used for their own ends. In both millennia exiles led the way: their lifestyle was the price for change; their discomfort the church's hope.

5

Exiles in the second millennium

By the thirteenth century the Roman paradigm of church history, which was in its infancy at the time of Pope Gregory the Great and lasted to the Reformation, was well formed and indeed on the brink of decline. The Protestant paradigm and the Enlightenment paradigm would follow in the sixteenth and eighteenth century respectively. And as we have seen, the postmodern world would begin in the 1960s. During the final centuries of the Roman paradigm exiles would lead the way in the renewal and reformation of the mission and spirituality of the church. They were exiles in the sense that they would try to escape the structures of their own paradigm (or world) and protest against what was corrupt spiritually or materially in it. In the second millennium these types of exiles were to the fore: men and women who recognized the weaknesses or faults of what confronted them and sought either by the lifestyle (or faith-style) they adopted, or the protest they personally embodied, to change the dominant paradigm in which they lived. Once again over a period as long as a millennium it is only possible to pick out the most representative exiles who must inevitably speak for very many others; they are drawn from most European nations and their ideals were to spread across the Atlantic and then to Asia and Africa.

An Italian subversive

Some time in the autumn or early winter of 1205 Francis of Assisi gave up his quest to become a knight through military prowess in inter-city Italian wars and found himself praying before a crucifix in the small chapel of San Damiano outside Assisi, where he received a vision. God, he recalled, said to him, 'Francis, go and repair my house which you can see is all being destroyed' (Galli, 2002, p. 36). Having been confronted by his father Peter Bernadone, a rich cloth merchant with more worldly ambitions for his son, Francis was put under a kind of house arrest. Later he was charged by his father before the local bishop with stealing his property, albeit with the laudable intention of restoring the chapel at San Damiano. Told to restore to his father any of his father's property which he still possessed, Francis in a dramatic gesture not only gave all he had back to his father but stripped off the clothes he stood in and returned them as well, standing naked before the court. It was an act of complete renunciation and poverty which was a sign of things to come (Galli, 2002, p. 41).

On 24 February 1208, some two and half years later, hearing part of Matthew's Gospel read in which Jesus called his disciples to go out with no money, food or spare clothing, Francis changed his attire from that of a hermit to a simple brown robe designed for a barefoot preacher. The order of mendicant friars (brothers) was all but begun. Joined by a few others, Francis wrote a brief rule in 1209 in which vows of poverty, simplicity and humility were central. The community was to have no possessions and rely entirely on the offerings of others. The vision for the order was not simply the rebuilding of a solitary chapel, but the rebuilding of the whole house of God (the Roman Catholic Church) which was in danger of being destroyed by luxury, worldliness and corruption. It was to this mission and the preaching of repentance in the context of poverty that Francis and his followers committed themselves.

Only a year later one of the most unlikely meetings in the history of Christendom took place between this simple friar, the 'poverello' in his brown habit, and the most powerful man in the Western world, Pope Innocent III. Innocent was close to calling the Fourth Lateran Council which would despatch the Fourth Crusade (which led to the disastrous sacking of Constantinople), and which began the persecution of attrition against the Albigensians (neo-Manichaean Cathars) in Southern France (Küng, 1995, pp. 399, 400) and the Waldensians, a group based on the espousal of biblical preaching conducted by lay preachers. Recognizing some of the weaknesses of the church and the need for spiritual renewal at a time when the papacy had embarked on a policy of extending its power and taking on its opponents, Innocent was prepared to patronize this new movement. He had the wit to recognize that what the realpolitik of papal power would fail to achieve, this new movement might accomplish. But Francis' work was clearly circumscribed from the start.

Innocent gave Francis permission to act as a penitential preaching order on condition that he did not question any of the Roman orders. In giving his allegiance to the Pope he was given freedom to operate, but at the cost of conformity to the Roman paradigm, which in turn protected his order. So what began as a subversive movement bent on radical spiritual renewal and discipleship became eventually a part of the panoply of spiritual medieval direction orchestrated from Rome. As Küng says, 'had Francis' demands, which were so in keeping with the gospel, been understood they could have powerfully put in question the centralised, legalised, politicised, militarised and clericalised Roman system, which had taken over the cause of Christ' (Küng, 1995, p. 412).

The Franciscan Order spread more rapidly than its sister Order, the Dominicans, which began at the same time and which was designed to combat heresy and teach the faith. However, what had begun as an exilic organization in the countryside south of Assisi soon became swallowed by the system. By 1230 the then Pope Gregory IX interpreted the vow of poverty to mean that although the friars could not own anything, they were nevertheless allowed something's use, a semantic difference which allowed them to own in all but name, which Francis had refused to do. A way of life had been inspired by Francis, a freedom exemplified by separation from the material and the worldly, a kind of exile had been advocated that shone brightly across the centuries, and a new form of spirituality had been engendered. But in terms of bringing a lasting shift to a system that was already in decline it failed; what started as subversive ended by being assimilated. Its willingness to comply with Innocent's terms meant that the followers of this truly radical disciple of Jesus would in the end be subverted by the system they had come to change.

The English exiles

A century later in England there was a stirring of a new spirituality which in time would coincide with a movement of reform, begun in Germany and later known as the Reformation. Three men who lived between the fourteenth and sixteenth centuries could justifiably claim the title exile, although each of their lives was quite different. One took himself outside the normal way of life by becoming a hermit; the second was an Oxford academic and government servant whose theology and call for reform of church doctrine in the end got him a kind of exile, albeit in Lutterworth, Leicestershire. The third vowed to translate the Scriptures into English so that any ploughboy would know more theology than the pope. These three were Richard Rolle, John Wycliffe and William Tyndale respectively.

Richard Rolle, a Yorkshireman from Pickering, is the least well known. Born in 1300, he broke off his studies and became a hermit under the patronage of William Neville, Archdeacon of Durham. For thirty years he lived the life of a hermit on his friend John Dalton's estate in Yorkshire until finally settling near a Cistercian monastery at Hampole, near Doncaster. Although he had no contact with a new movement of European creativity, he wrote at a time of flowering of spiritual and more secular literature in Europe. Living a little after Dante in Florence but at the same time as Petrarch and Boccaccio, and before Geoffrey Chaucer, he was contemporary with a great period of creativity in writing and expression. He was also part of a flowering of English mystical and devotional writing at that time; chief among those who produced it were Walter Hilton, Mother Julian of Norwich, Margery Kempe and the anonymous author of *The Cloud of Unknowing*. Their writings seem to reflect a comparable and contemporaneous mystical movement in the Orthodox Church called Hesychasm (from the Greek *hesychia*, inner stillness) in which a person sought inner stillness through use of the Jesus Prayer and a greater apprehension of God. This type of mystical approach in prayer, advanced also by the English mystics, was being defended in the East by St Gregory Palamas (1296–1359), Archbishop of Thessalonica (Ware, 1997, pp. 61ff). Among many other writings, Rolle composed lyric poems, mystical and devotional writing, as well as commentaries on Scripture and translations of the Psalms. His knowledge of the Bible was extensive and he chose to write in English as well as in Latin, creating a precedent for translators nearly two centuries later. 'His knowledge of the scriptures was profound, and with pardonable idealism he expected a deep knowledge of scripture among all people of religion' (Lampe, 1975, p. 386). But it is for his devotional and mystical writing that he is best known. This example of his devotional writing, which is about experiencing God's love, shows why:

I cannot tell you how surprised I was the first time I felt my heart begin to warm. It was real warmth too, not imaginary, and it felt as if it were actually on fire. I was astonished at the way the heat surged up, and how this new sensation brought great and unexpected comfort, I had to keep feeling my breast to make sure there was no physical reason for it! But once I realized that it came entirely from within, that this fire of love had no cause, material or sinful, but was the gift of my Maker, I was absolutely delighted, and wanted my love to be even greater. And this longing was all the more urgent because of the delightful effect and interior sweetness which this spiritual flame fed into my soul, so sweet was the devotion it kindled.

(The Fire of Love, prologue)

No wonder his scriptural understanding and devotional experience proved formative in the growing desire to regain a genuine spirituality for the English people.

Wycliffe was a very different man. Known to Edward III's sons the Black Prince and John of Gaunt, he was a leading academic and public servant. He was Master of Balliol College and later Warden of Canterbury Hall (which later became known as Christ Church) founded by Cardinal Wolsey. He represented the Crown in negotiations with the Papal Curia from 1374 to 1378. At the same time he was impatient with clerical corruption and the dependence of the church on superstition, the theory of 'transubstantiation' in which the body and blood in the Communion service changed into the actual body and blood of Jesus, in 'substance' (inner significance) if not in 'accident' (outward appearance) according to Aristotelian categories. He drew from Scripture the notion of one true and universal church made up of faithful disciples, which was known only to God. With his attack, in uncompromising terms, on the monastic way of life in *Apostasia* he made many enemies, especially among the friars, and although protected by John of Gaunt he was forced to leave Oxford in 1381. He died in Lutterworth three years later, but while there he gave support to his followers for the translation of the Bible. His secretary John Purvey completed a further translation of the Bible in 1396 of which 200 manuscripts are still in existence today (Lampe, 1975, p. 388). Wycliffe's work lived on through the preaching of the Lollards (a Flemish term of abuse for preachers whom they called mumblers), and among the more revolutionary elements of English society present in the Peasants' Revolt led by Wat Tyler in 1381. Partly because the anticlericalism in Wycliffe's writings fuelled the social upheavals in the early part of Richard II's reign, both the Lollards' and Wycliffe's own writings and translations were suppressed. But his influence had spread to the Continent where in Prague Hus took up his ideals, and still today in the Czech Republic churches are named after Wycliffe. But in 1415 at the Council of Constance both Lollards and the Husites were condemned. Hus himself was burnt and the new King Henry V was more interested in gaining the support of his clergy, whom he called up for military service to claim the crown of France, than in airing the complaints of Wycliffe's followers. Realpolitik once again trumped any desire for reform. Like many who followed him, Wycliffe was prepared to go outside the accepted norms of religion to bring his countrymen back to the teaching and practice of the Bible.

However, the third exile, who was born around a century after Wycliffe's death, set in train the greatest change to English spirituality, and arguably more than anyone put in place the most influential building block of English nationhood. William Tyndale was born in or near to 1494, and just 42 years later was burnt at the stake in Belgium. His 'crime' was the translation of the Bible into English. Like Wycliffe he studied at Oxford, at Magdalen College and in 1522 he conceived of the project of translating the Bible into English, building on the work of Wycliffe and his followers. But his proposal was given a cool response by Bishop Tunstall and Sir Thomas More. So to complete his work he left for the Continent where four years previously the Reformation had begun. The completed English New Testament was printed at Worms and then taken back to England where its arrival was opposed by Archbishop Warham, Tunstall and More. They regarded the translation as a Trojan horse for Protestantism; replacing words like 'do penance' with 'repentance'; 'church' with 'congregation' and 'priest' with 'elder' (Lampe, 1975, p. 145). And it was around such traditional words that the whole Roman system had been built up; to change these words risked jeopardizing the whole edifice. Tyndale's Bible was revolutionary in its effect. In 1534 Henry VIII's break with Rome, on account of his divorce from Katherine of Aragon, made England fertile ground for the growth of Protestantism. With the aid of the printing press, 1,600 copies of Tyndale's translation had been circulated in England by the time of his death. In a population of 2.5 million this was a significant number. And by 1539

Thomas Cromwell persuaded Henry to have an English Bible placed in every parish church, and by 1541 it was an offence not to do so (MacCulloch, 2003, p. 203). Almost miraculously just five years after his martyrdom, every parish church had a copy of the English Bible, called the King's Bible. Tyndale's Bible was the basis of all subsequent English Bibles up to the twentieth century. Completed in exile, it ended the exclusion of the English nation from the text of the Scriptures and it mirrored what had already happened in Germany through the titanic struggles of Martin Luther.

The German prophet

On 16 April 1521 Martin Luther arrived at Worms from Wittenberg in a simple agricultural cart. He was greeted by around two thousand townsfolk, declaring as he alighted, 'God will be with me.' The following day he was to appear before the Emperor Charles V, the most powerful ruler in the Western world, not to debate the teaching that he had proposed, as he had done previously at Augsburg and Leipzig, but rather to face a formal command by the Emperor to recant. Already Pope Leo X, a Medici, keener on hunting than prayer, had served notice on his teaching by issuing the bull of excommunication, *Exsurge Domine.* Luther had publicly burnt the Bull together with many books on canon law. He now stood trial before the Emperor and was expected to retract his condemnation of papal power and his teaching condemning the sale of indulgences, the superstition of relics, as well as his teaching about the sacraments and the theology of penance and justification by faith. But Luther refused, uttering the famous words:

> Unless I am convinced by the testimony of the scriptures, or by clear reason (for I do not trust either the Pope or in Councils alone, since it is well known that they have often erred and contradicted themselves), I am bound by the scriptures I have quoted and my conscience is captive to the word of God. I cannot and I will not retract anything, since it is neither safe nor right to go against conscience.

The next day he was branded a heretic. He was given 21 days to return to Wittenberg and to desist from all preaching. On his return journey he was spirited away by friends into a sturdy fortress at Wartburg. An exile in his own land, Luther immediately began the translation of Erasmus's Greek New Testament into German.

By 1534 he had produced a complete translation of the Bible, being proficient in Greek and Hebrew. While he was hidden at Wartburg, he must have reviewed his tempestuous life thus far.

Against his father's wish that he would be a lawyer, Luther – having had two narrow escapes from death – offered himself as a friar at an Augustinian friary at Erfurt. His first celebration of Mass as a priest was a forbidding moment. He had a scrupulous conscience, was often plagued by doubt and was prone throughout his life to depression or *Anfechtungen* (assault on the soul, see Tomlin, 2002, p. 41). In particular Luther wrestled with the teaching of the day to find any assurance of salvation. He found no respite from his struggles in any of the following: the narrow scholasticism based on the works of Aquinas and the schoolmen; the new teaching (or *via moderna*) of William of Ockham, which did not espouse the idea of universal precepts advocated in the writings of Aquinas and Duns Scotus (the *via antiqua*): the humanist search of the classics as exemplified by Erasmus or the endless round of spiritual duties expected by monastic life. Encouraged by his spiritual director he increasingly focused on the sufferings of Christ. But it was precisely because Luther held on to his doubts long enough, waiting for real answers that satisfied him at every level, intellectual, moral and emotional, that God was able to break through with those answers which were demonstrably based on Scripture as well as being able to transform.

In 1508 he was appointed to the chair of moral theology in Wittenberg. A small town but with a large collection of relics, in fact 5,005, including nine thorns from Christ's crown of thorns as well as phials of the Virgin's milk! (Atkinson, 1965, p. 61). The collective value in terms of time remitted from purgatory for penitents who visited them (and paid) was according to medieval calculation 127,709 years and 116 days. Such practices together with a preaching of an indulgence in his area by Tetzel and Luther's own visit to Rome provoked his protest against the papacy and Curia and resulted in his nailing his 95 theses on the castle church door in Wittenberg in 1517. They amounted to a gauntlet being thrown down against the practice of the time of selling indulgences (which, crudely speaking, bought time off from purgatory) and a challenge to the authority of the pope. By then, after a long struggle, Luther had come to understand that the justifying grace of God that comes not from religious observance but from faith alone in the promise of God. But this did not become clear to him until after a prolonged spiritual struggle.

From 1512 onwards, when Luther first began lecturing on the Bible at Wittenberg, he struggled to understand the true meaning of the gospel. For two hours each week, beginning at 6 a.m., he lectured his way through the book of Psalms. While much of his teaching was in line with the so-called *via moderna*, the new method of teaching popular in the universities, Luther showed from the Psalms that God can give his grace and gifts to people who are suffering, humbled and contrite. Nor was the grace of God solely dependent on the ministry of the church, but could be encountered directly by the individual sinner, as David frequently did in the psalms. But it was while teaching on Romans, and in particular on Romans 1.17 that Luther understood that the phrase 'the righteousness of God' did not mean the punishing righteousness of God, but rather the righteous-making power of God for all who believe. This insight was like a window opening in heaven as he understood that righteousness was a gift received by faith and not a status conferred by the church for fulfilment of religious duties. No longer were adoration of relics, pilgrimages, the purchase of indulgences or attendance at masses needed as steps towards salvation; rather only personal faith in Christ's redemptive work, leading to justification, was required. As Küng says, 'The rediscovery of the original Pauline message of justification under the shifts and over-paintings of 1500 years is an amazing, a tremendous theological achievement' (Küng, 1995, p. 534). It was Luther's own personal quest for assurance and for relief for his own conscience, in conjunction with his remarkable forensic skills as a biblical interpreter, tethered to a stubborn courage, which meant that what he discovered he would make known at all costs. This powerful amalgam provided the springboard for the Reformation. No wonder he stressed *solus Christus*, *sola gratia*, s*ola scriptura* and *sola fides* as the four-sided basis of the new paradigm shift. The tragedy was that although he wanted to be a reforming Catholic, he was excommunicated (Atkinson, 1965, p. 73). Not unlike John Wesley, another reformer in a different century, he was forced out into a kind of exile, as Wesley's followers were later, and this was the cost Luther paid for the reformation he brought. Luther could no longer stray outside the protection of Protestant rulers. He was *persona non grata* in the Roman Catholic world. He did not have the temperament to work for reconciliation, nor would any overtures have been accepted. The most irenic of the Reformers, Melancthon, tried at the Colloquy of Ratisbon in 1541, but too much had been said by then on both sides to hope for any kind of rapprochement.

Nor could Luther meet all the aspirations he had unleashed. When peasants rebelled against their rulers in 1525 Luther did not come to their aid. The realpolitik of the situation was that Luther and Protestantism needed the support of Protestant rulers without whose patronage they would be overwhelmed by Catholic power. The history of Europe for the next two hundred years was enshrined in the principal *cuius regio, eius religio*, meaning the religion of the king is the religion of the people, literally 'whose rule, his religion'. As far as Luther was concerned, social justice came very much second to the need for religious protection and the advancement of Protestantism; in exchange for this Protestants must, for the time being, accept a degree of social inequality. Nor could Luther prevent the Reformation going further than he intended as different views of the sacraments sprang up and defined new Protestant communities such as the Baptists. For many the Reformation he brought was only a halfway house; they looked for social justice, pacifism in place of the compulsion that had characterized the Roman system and a new understanding of the sacraments. No one represented this nexus of convictions better than the Mennonites, another movement that had to weather exile if it was to survive and make its own distinctive contribution.

Although Luther hoped to be able to reform the Roman system from the inside, his excommunication did not mean that the Catholic Church was impervious to change. New spiritual movements were about to begin which proved very powerful. While loyal to the pope and antagonistic to Luther, once the politics of religion was removed (which was impossible at the time), these movements had much in common. The tragedy was they were not appraised for their intrinsic spiritual merit but for where they sided in the confessional antipathies of the times. This attitude continued for the best part of four hundred years; but today you might find a Lutheran going on an Ignatian retreat or an evangelical talking about 'the dark night of the soul'. They would be using spiritual disciplines which developed in sixteenth-century Catholic mysticism, and to their contribution in particular we must now turn.

Two mystics and a mathematician

If Luther brought reformation to Europe he did so not only to the so-called Protestant churches defined by their protest against Rome but he also provoked change in Roman Catholicism itself. First, there was a reappraisal of Roman Catholic doctrine by the Council of Trent and second, there was a growth of a new more rigorous and focused Catholic spirituality as pioneered by Ignatius of Loyola. Another soldier turned mystic, Ignatius Loyola wrote his *Spiritual Exercises* (published in Rome in 1541) and founded the Society of Jesus, the Jesuits. If poverty had been the watchword for Francis, now obedience was the watchword for Ignatius. For Ignatius 'obedience to a superior is the condition of a soldierly service of God and a total self-abnegation in the individual' (O. Chadwick, 1973, p. 258). Not a little 'exilic' himself, although committed like his companion Francis Xavier to disciplined but pragmatic mission in obedience to the papacy, Ignatius provided the setting in which others like him sought a more radical dependence on God, not the least of these are two Spanish mystics whose lives and writings bear testimony to their passion for exile, Teresa of Avila and John of the Cross.

Teresa, the beautiful daughter of a rich merchant of Avila, Don Alonso, was both passionate and sensitive by nature. One of nine children from his second marriage, she had seven brothers and a sister, Juana. At the age of seven, displaying her feisty and romantic nature, she determined to go to the land of the Moors with a boy called Rodrigo and there become a martyr; they got only as far as a mile from home (du Boulay, 1991, p. 21). After an initially unsuccessful time at an Augustinian convent in Avila she joined the Carmelites, an order based on the experiences of Elijah on Mount Carmel. But while dangerously ill and staying with her uncle Don Pedro she was introduced to the works of Francis of Osuna, a spiritual writer well known for his work *The Third Spiritual Alphabet*, later banned by the Inquisition. Words from the opening chapter had a profound effect on her. She read, 'Friendship and communion with God are possible in the life of *exile*. This friendship is not remote but more sure and intimate than ever existed between brothers or even between mother and child' (du Boulay, 1991, p. 22). Coming as it did soon after the death of her own mother, it offered profound hope and aspiration, an aspiration, however, which, in terms of prayer and experience, was not realized for many years, in fact not until her early forties. Only then does she write about prayer which had resulted from her own abandonment and her apprehension of God's transforming presence. Teresa describes four stages of prayer resulting in what she describes as the Prayer of Union, following which 'she found her-self in a state of overwhelming tenderness, bathed in tears of joy. Sometimes it was only these tears, something she valued deeply, which convinced her she had not been dreaming. She felt humble, full of courage, able to make heroic promises and was beginning to abhor the world' (du Boulay, 1991, p. 41). Fortified by this prayer, by mentors from the Jesuit order, she withstood the banning of Osuna's book by the Inquisition in 1559 and criticism from her own order and set about founding a new reformed Carmelite order both stricter in discipline and more devoted to prayer, which prayer she now described as 'friendly intercourse, and frequent solitary converse, with him who we know loves us' (du Boulay, 1991, p. 58). In 1567 Teresa had her first meeting with a diminutive but highly impressive Carmelite called John of the Cross.

There has been much debate about the validity and authenticity of Christian mysticism. Is it part of the discipleship that Christ commanded? Where might the practice of mystical prayer be found in the Scriptures? Perhaps in Paul's experiences which he alluded to but would not speak of (e.g. 2 Corinthians 12.1–4) or Jesus' temptations in the wilderness. Indeed Küng writes: 'What did Jesus require of people? Extraordinary ecstatic experiences, ruminating speculation about God's nature, psychological self-dissection and unhistorical techniques of immersion? No, love of God and love of neighbour' (Küng, 1995, p. 449). Despite their inherent danger of becoming a 'self-work', mystical experiences abound in all quarters of the church, and none more so than in the life of John of the Cross. Perhaps it would be true to say that if mysticism is an end in itself it can become a snare, but if it is a charism or gift in prayer, then it becomes a blessing. Teresa wrote of her own path of prayer in *The Way of Perfection*, *The Foundations* and *The Interior Castle*. John of the Cross also wrote about prayer, in the form of commentaries on three of his own poems, *The Spiritual Canticle*, *The Dark Night* and *The Living Flame of Love*. John writes of the God who gives himself; the space we make for this gift, the opening God himself carves in us to make room for the gift; and the development of faith that stretches from God's plan in eternity to its final fulfilment in heaven (see Matthew, 1995, p. 114). Perhaps the heart of what he is saying is conveyed best by the more homely message that

> When you are burdened you are joined to God. He is your strength, and he is with people who suffer. When there is no burden, you are just with yourself, your own weakness. It is in difficulties which test our patience that the virtue and strength of the soul is increased and affirmed.　　　　　(Matthew, 1995, p. 78, quoting *Sayings* 40)

And the way to travel along this pilgrimage of prayer is through faith, love and hope in, for and through Christ (Matthew, 1995, p. 94). For John the night was symbolized and experienced by his own imprisonment in a dark hole in Toledo for seeking the reform of his Order. But night for him was both a place of suffering and a place of grace, a night of beatitude or sheer grace, in Spanish, 'Oh dichosa ventura' ('O venture of delight!') (Matthew, 1995, p. 54). The way to this grace was contemplation, for 'contemplation is nothing but a hidden, peaceful, loving inflow of God. If it is given room, it will inflame the spirit with love' (*The Dark Night* Book One, 10.6). And if mentors are involved in helping the soul in this pathway, John wrote,

> Those who guide souls should realise that the principal agent and guide and motive force in this matter is not them, but the Holy Spirit, who never fails in his care of people; they are only instruments to guide people to perfection by faith and the law of God, according to the Spirit that God is giving to the individual person.
>
> (*The Living Flame of Love*, 3.46)

Suffused by a profound knowledge of Scripture, imbibing the concept of Jesus as 'lover of my soul', he provided at once the most comprehensive explanation of spirituality through the poetic medium, dwelling, as Luther did in his theology of the cross, on the greatest test of our discipleship being suffering, or in John's words 'the night of the soul'.

It is interesting to contrast these two Catholic mystics existing at the height of Catholic Spain's power (both for a time suspected at least and temporarily spurned by their own tradition) with a brilliant

Frenchman of nearly a century later. He was also drawn to the Augustinian view of human beings which stressed their sinfulness as well as their own spiritual impotence. Whereas in Spain this existed, in part at least, among the Discalced Carmelites of which John was a leader, a century later in France this Augustinianism re-emerged at the French convent of Port-Royal in Paris. One of its chief advocates was a brilliant mathematician, Blaise Pascal and the movement he was associated with was Jansenism.

A French family called the Arnaulds were highly influential in this movement. In 1602, at the age of ten, Angélique Arnauld was appointed Abbess of Port-Royal and over the following years it became a place of powerful spiritual influence. Her brother Antoine, a theologian and philosopher, also relied heavily on Augustine's teachings. Mixing with the highly influential Saint-Cyran and Cornelius Jansen, a Dutch 'Calvinist', he set out to refute the Jesuits whose views, as expressed through the teacher Molina, stressed the freedom of human will and the ability to cooperate with God. In many ways it was a kind of Catholic preview of the great debates between Arminianism and Calvinism which were to divide eighteenth-century evangelicals in England. Into this circle Jacqueline Pascal was drawn and she became a member of the Port-Royal community. It was directed by Saint-Cyran, Jansen's associate and its Abbess for many years was Antoine Arnauld's sister, Angélique. It always had at best an uneasy relationship with the Catholic hierarchy in France and despite an accord arranged in the Peace of the Church in 1668 was eventually suppressed in 1709. Jacqueline Pascal strongly influenced her brother, Blaise, the great mathematician. (At the age of 16 he presented his first paper on conic sections, later invented a calculating machine to help his father collect taxes for the government in Normandy where he was the Intendent, demonstrated the concept of a vacuum, and was a friend of Fermat and acquaintance of the older Descartes.) Pascal was not unlike William Wilberforce, full of gaiety and wit, not at all averse in early years to gambling but troubled by a sensitive conscience and member of a circle which was interested in searching out spiritual truth. Famously on Monday 23 November 1654 he had an intense encounter with God. Although he said nothing about this in his lifetime a full testimony to that night was written out and sewn into his cloak only to be found after his death. He wrote about that night as follows:

The year of grace 1654

Monday, 23 November, the feast of St. Clement, pope and martyr, and of others in the martyrology.

The Vigil of St. Chrysogonus, martyr, and others.

From about half past ten at night until about half past midnight.

FIRE

GOD of Abraham, GOD of Isaac, GOD of Jacob

Not the God of the philosophers and of the learned.

Certitude. Certitude. Feeling. Joy. Peace.

GOD of Jesus Christ.

Deum meum et Deum vostrum (My God and your God) [John 20.17]

Your GOD will be my God. [Ruth 1.16]

Forgetfulness of the world and of everything, except GOD

He can only be found by the ways taught in the Gospel.

Grandeur of the human soul.

Righteous Father, the world has not known you, but I have known you. [John 17.25]

Joy, joy, joy, tears of joy.

(Connor, 2006, p. 148)

Pascal now took to defending Port-Royal, Antoine Arnauld and the now deceased but influential Saint-Cyran. Soon after the first of his satirical *Provincial Letters* appeared; they were published in their entirety posthumously. But the authorities were gunning for any appearance of Jansenism. Port-Royal was later suppressed and the Abbey was destroyed. Pascal died, having suffered all his life from ill health, and Antoine was officially degraded and banished. This form of Catholicism was in effect exiled. The reign of Louis XIV was soon under way and the Edict of Nantes, which had given Protestants freedom of worship, was revoked. A period of state Roman Catholic hegemony began, ended only by the French Revolution and the birth of the rationalist movement in France. Pascal together with the Arnauld family had stood out against the centralizing tendency of the French state led by Cardinals Richelieu and Mazarin. They stood for the freedom to respond to God according to the grace that God gave rather than by obedience to the teachings and discipline of the church. They were exiles willing to fight for the need for an encounter with God based on his grace as being the touchstone of true Christian discipleship. This was the recorded experience that Pascal had sewn into his cloak and which went with him wherever he went.

A firebrand from Lincolnshire

Across the channel in England some forty years later on 9 February 1709, a five-year-old John Wesley was snatched from his father's burning rectory. Wesley's life covered almost the whole of the eighteenth century. Together with Whitefield – from whom he broke in 1741 over the subject of Calvinism and human free will to respond to the gospel – they were, under God, responsible for the Great Awakening, which was an unprecedented revival in England seen neither before nor since. Owen Chadwick says that the rules of the Holy Club which Wesley founded while a student at Christ Church were more rigorous than Ignatius Loyola's *Spiritual Exercises*, and Wesley a more autocratic leader than Ignatius (O. Chadwick, 1973, p. 259). As Wesley's father said of him, 'He will have a reason for everything he has to do. I suppose he will not even break wind, unless he had a reason for it' (Tomkins, 2003, p. 15). With his father's stubbornness and intransigence and his mother Susanna's energy, organizational skills and piety, John was likely to be unusual but his 17 siblings, apart from Charles, the prolific and much-loved hymn writer, never rivalled him for greatness. But it was a combination of the German gospel insight of the Moravian brothers and the Spirit's direction that enabled Wesley to find the grace that evaded him in the Holy Club and that could yield true righteousness and salvation. It was when reading the works of the Moravian Brethren from East Germany from the estate of Count Zinzendorf along with the Preface of Luther's commentary on Romans that Wesley's heart was 'strangely warmed'. While listening to a reading from this commentary, Wesley's heart gained a liberation and assurance that enabled him to begin his prodigious ministry. But when he subsequently asked for permission from bishops to preach in their churches he was refused, one bishop referring to his faith as a 'horrid enthusiasm'. The truth was that much of the Church of England was overrun by rationalism or deism and its comfortable social order wanted no rocking. Wesley was banished to preach in the fields and other public places – a form of exile. The crowds he preached to were enormous and the supernatural accompaniment to his preaching was extraordinary. The world was his parish and for the next forty years he travelled annually an average of eight thousand miles, preaching wherever he could. A wave of lay pastors was created in the wake of his meetings; they cared for the newly converted people in the strict method that he laid down and whom he called together in an annual conference. Although Wesley died a loyal Anglican and received the sacrament every day, his followers did not feel so attached to the Church of England, nor were they welcome, so Methodism was quickly formed as a separate movement and church.

Wesley had laid the spiritual basis for social and missionary changes. His concern for the poor led him naturally to condemn slavery and give unequivocal support to Wilberforce in the movement for the abolition of the slave trade. His own evangelistic fervour gave impetus to the missionary movement that would accompany the expansion of the British Empire in the nineteenth century. His intellectual gifts, energy and perseverance were commonly recognized so that by the end of his life he was widely admired; the preacher who was exiled to the fields began a spiritual movement which in the next hundred years would grow and grow.

The home of exiles

Perhaps one country more than any other used exile as a way of controlling its population – that country was Russia. Whether tsars or communists were in charge, Siberia and the gulags were ready to receive those whom either regime perceived as dissidents.

After the fall of Constantinople Moscow had become 'The Third Rome'. The tsars and the Orthodox Church agreed a classic pact in which each lent credibility and power to the other: the tsars were revered as virtually divine, and the liturgy of the Orthodox Church became the cradle of Russian hopes and aspirations (Figes, 2001, pp. 296, 297). These attitudes were only strengthened by the vicissitudes of Russian history and life. But by the mid nineteenth century the Orthodox Church, and in particular its rural priesthood, were mired in poverty and illiteracy; renewal and reform were needed, and once again this came through a spiritual community.

Two hundred kilometres south of Moscow was the monastery of Optina Pustyn, originally founded in the fourteenth century. For around sixty years from 1829 to 1891 three great leaders, themselves disciples of a previous spiritual leader, Father Paissy, led its spiritual revival and influence in Russian life: they were Father Leonid, Father

Marky and Father Amvrosy (Figes, 2001, p. 294). It was to them that the giants of Russian literature repaired: Gogol, Dostoevsky and Tolstoy. Gogol wrote to Tolstoy,

> I stopped at the hermitage at Optina and took away with me a memory that will never fade. Clearly grace dwells in that place. You can feel it even in the outward signs of worship. Nowhere have I seen monks like these. Through every one of them I seemed to converse with heaven.
>
> (Figes, 2001, p. 310)

While in exile for his socialist views Dostoevsky recalled the inspiration encountered at Optina, as well as his conversations with peasants who for him embodied the redemptive quality of the Russian soul. When Tolstoy was dying he bought a railway ticket for Kozelsk (the station for Optina) so that he could wait for death in the peace of its surroundings. No country in the world could boast such a collection of writers whose works were to have profound worldwide significance and who derived such inspiration from a single source. Most of them, as virtual outsiders, wrote about the disintegration of Russian society burdened by church and autocratic government while itself still using a moribund bureaucratic system bulging with its own agents. When the tsarist censor, so quick in earlier times to censor Pushkin, overlooked the publication of Marx's *Das Kapital* and its first print run of 3,000 sold out, ferment began to take hold among the liberal middle classes and urban factory-workers. The First World War and an isolated Tsar and family hastened the descent to Revolution. When the Revolution came and Christian faith and the Tsarist government were outlawed, a whole, vast new group of exiles was created, both in Russia and later in the Communist block of Eastern European countries.

Space will not let us recall these exiles but for seventy years until 1989, Russia was dominated by its Communist leaders and doctrines while the church was divided between those who silently accommodated the Communist government and those who were sent to the gulags. Writing in blistering words of the head of the Russian Orthodox Church, Patriarch Pimen, in 1972, Solzhenitsyn said of the church's accommodation:

> By what reasoning is it possible to convince oneself that the planned destruction of the spirit and body of the church under the guidance

of atheists is the best way of *preserving* it? Preserving it for whom? Certainly not for Christ. Preserving it by what means? By falsehood. But after the falsehood by whose hands are the holy mysteries to be celebrated? (quoted in Beeson, 1974, p. 73)

There is more than echo here of the Donatist controversy in North Africa in the third century. The anguished reply of Father Zhelukov to this onslaught on behalf of Pimen, who had chosen not to speak out, was

What can we do in such a situation? Say: all or nothing? Attempt to go underground, something unthinkable under a regime of this kind? Or again, subscribe in some way to the system and exploit the possibilities which are still permitted? (Beeson, 1974, p. 73)

Here we have the dilemma in every age: the 'discretion' of 'exploiting the opportunities', or the 'valour' of confronting it from exile. Elsewhere in Europe other leaders went into exile: Cardinal Mindszenty, the leader of the Hungarian Catholics, for 15 years lived in the American Embassy in Budapest; Cardinal Wyszynski was imprisoned in a monastery in 1953 and Cardinal Slipyj of the Ukrainian Catholic Church was imprisoned for 17 years until 1963, when he was exiled to Rome, occasionally wearing his prison clothes to advertise the suffering of his church at home, which, he said, had lost ten million members through war, starvation and persecution (O. Chadwick, 1992, pp. 53, 54). In Russia and Eastern Europe, exile was the price of change and survival.

Over the previous two chapters we have seen that the history of the church, and society in Europe, since Jesus has been divided into five great paradigms, each of which came to determine the attitudes and aspirations of the recognized leaders of the Christian communities in their own period. The Apostolic church gave way to the Greek Church largely based in the Near East until it in turn gave way, in the West to the Roman paradigm from the sixth century onwards. Only in the sixteenth century did that finally break up under the weight of its own corruption and the spiritual force of Luther and the Reformers. The Reformers went back to the original text of Scripture to rediscover the gospel. This in turn led to a reformation of Catholicism, a period of bitter and bloody struggle in Europe which gave way eventually to the next paradigm, of the Enlightenment. This reason-based paradigm developed for three hundred years alongside the renewal of the church especially, in England, in the eighteenth century, which led to a worldwide missionary movement. But as each paradigm gave way to the next, the renewal of the church to a large extent depended on these exiles.

In the first millennium many of these exiles were involved in contending for Christian truth not least the divinity of Christ and the definition of the Trinity, the most notable being Athanasius. After the fall of Rome and the long stretch of the Dark Ages the monastic ideal, with Benedict's Rule prevailing, provided a model of community in the West which was both detached from the world but at the same time committed to its transformation – this too was a kind of exile. In Northern Europe Celtic Christianity was committed to a form of evangelism and was centred off-shore and resourced by strong community life.

By contrast the exiles of the second millennium were to a greater or lesser extent protest movements over against a paradigm which had replaced service by power and truth with vested interest. Some, like the Franciscans, were radical at first but later were enfolded by the paradigm which at first Francis had nobly challenged. Others sought isolation to develop a more authentic and sincere spiritual life. Many were driven to research the foundation of true faith in the Scriptures by understanding the original languages of the Bible and publishing the Bible in the vernacular. Such were Luther and Tyndale who made making the Gospel available in German and English. And when the church was synonymous with the state as in Louis XIV's France or Georgian England, to bring renewal or indeed revival meant going outside the church as did Port-Royal, Wesley and many others like the Puritans.

Now we are at another great shift where the enlightened modern world based on rationalism has given way to a new paradigm in its early stages of development. For the past two centuries until the 1960s Christianity and scientific rationalism have struggled together (with the church sometimes timidly giving up her distinctive message to reason) but now in the pluralist, postmodern society it appears that Christendom's days are over. It is more a case of the church returning to its apostolic roots but in a different way, conscious of its own exilic vocation, aware of its weakness and no longer having a seat at

·the table of the state. So if this is its own freshly minted exilic status, having lost the clothes of office, how does this affect its spirituality, its way of mission, and how can it 'sing the Lord's song in a strange land'? To these questions we must finally turn.

6

Attitudes and spirituality for an exiled church

Before going any further, it is time to pull together some of the threads of the argument of this book. The theme of exile figured strongly in the history of the people of God in Old Testament times, and also, to a degree, in New Testament times. In the Old Testament exile was a physical reality, the removal of the bulk of a nation to a foreign land where they were to live for at least 70 years. In the New Testament exile described that sense of being distanced from surrounding culture because Christian communities sensed that they belonged elsewhere, that heaven was their home and from there they awaited a Saviour who would fulfil their longings for the Kingdom of God to be fully made known.

In the history of Israel exile was never far from the consciousness of the nation; after all they were descended from a wandering Aramean. At the time of their Exodus, the children of Israel spent forty years journeying in the desert before reaching the Promised Land. Failure to follow the law carried with it the warning that they would be scattered among the nations and, despite the strictures of the prophets and the fate of the Northern Kingdom – whose rebellious ways were punished by deportation by the Assyrians and the re-settlement of the land by a mixed group of races – Judah persisted in ignoring the warnings of the prophets, not least Jeremiah. Eventually they were taken into captivity as both a punishment for their stubborn refusal to change and follow God's ways, as well as for their persistent idolatry. Exile, like many punishments, was both penal and remedial. It provided a very uncomfortable wake-up call for Judah's years of disobedience, as well as an opportunity for radical change in which the vocation of Israel, the vision of Israel and the dependency of Israel on YHWH was deeply reworked in circumstances of great vulnerability. In exile all the familiar supports of Temple, priesthood, ritual and feasts were more or less gone. By the waters of Babylon the chosen people had to work out both their past (what had gone wrong?) and their future (what was God's purpose for them now?). The two great prophets who were there to help them were Isaiah (Second Isaiah) and Ezekiel. And in second Isaiah we have the complete restating and recasting of God's redemptive purpose for them, and through them for the world. Once again the community, now a community of exiles, was fashioned and formed by the divine word coming to them at a time of great weakness and receptivity. As we hear this story again, so central to the whole Old Testament narrative, we ask are there any echoes here of the church's own situation today in Britain?

The second thread to pick up is the theme that the church in Britain faces a kind of exile today. We have seen the reasons for this: the decline if not implosion of Christendom with only a fragile legacy remaining, much dependent in our national life on the life and values of our present monarch; the pluralism and multiculturalism of society which makes government's role increasingly seen to be arbitrating between various religions without advocating any particular one; the decline of institutional church which is not yet offset by the rise of ethnic and new churches without whom the numerical decline of church life would be precipitate; the change of culture and philosophy, defined now as postmodern, which can accommodate almost all experience as truth (i.e. 'if it is true for you it is true', a philosophy at once as receptive and non-judgemental as it is superficial, an issue-skirting ideal to be sought as a kind of philosophical glue, provided it is not too severely tested); and last, the all-too-strident challenge of aggressive atheism, as peddled by the likes of Richard Dawkins and Sam Harris, who want to take potshots at fundamentalist stereotypes that most Christians in Britain would anyhow disown. Of course there are blips to this trend of alienation between church and society, such as the formidable record in education by church schools (at least four thousand of them), leading to a new form of nominalism of the kind expressed by would-be school parents, 'We'll get them done [i.e. baptized] to get them in'; the doubling of congregations at Christmas, especially in historic buildings, leaving the church with the task of welcoming half the Christmas worshippers but also trying to persuade them that 'God is for life and not just for Christmas!' (Not a few contemporary atheists or agnostics might agree with Dawkins that they would happily sing Christmas carols, not because they believed any of it but because they were content to be cultural Christians.) However, despite these welcome accolades for the quality of its education or the quality of its Christmas worship, for much of the time now the church feels itself in a kind of exile, which means that although it once had a chair at the table of government it is now left in the foyer, although it was once regarded as an authority in the land it is now only one among many voices, although its teaching and values were a defining feature of national heritage its leaders are one voice among many; although its tenets of faith or conduct were held in high regard, now some of these are traduced. It must therefore sing the Lord's song in an old land which has become strange. This need neither frighten nor frustrate the church but it does call us first to change our mentality or attitude and then change our ways, especially in terms of spirituality and mission.

The third thread to pick up from the preceding sections is quite simply that exile is the church's best friend. This does not mean that it is easy or without suffering or hardship but if a review of church history has shown us anything it is that exile has often been the price of change, renewal and at times revival. In the early centuries of the church's history it led an exilic life, it fully lived out the call in the New Testament to be exiles and strangers in the land and therefore to look elsewhere for its home. Down the years of church history men and women of exile provided the change that was necessary to uphold truth, to defy powerful systems, to challenge human-made philosophies and declare the gospel message in its essential form against the accretions of the church and to espouse a spirituality that was capable of reforming, or if necessary discarding, worn out and corrupt rituals that so easily take root. The thread from the history of the church over the past fifteen hundred years is that exile is often the price of renewal and of substantive change.

Taking these threads together, we can safely say that exile has often been part of God's plan for his people for their refinement and purging in order to concentrate their attention on their true vocation. We can further say that the church in Britain may be facing such a process both for its own good and for the advantage of the society to whom it witnesses. So exile, if embraced, is not to be feared, but is the means of renewal not in a moment, but over a period of time. And if we are in a kind of exile then adaptations must be made to our attitudes, our spirituality and our mission. The remainder of this chapter will consider the church's attitudes and spirituality in the light of this. The church's mission will be considered in the following chapter.

Fresh attitudes for an exiled church

Let's think for a moment of the Jewish exiles in Babylon, who had been forcefully taken from their homes and from the familiarity of their culture and religious institutions in Jerusalem and Judah. What changes of attitude must they have been through – from a complacency that thought that something would turn up to save them (as it had done when they were threatened by the Assyrians in 702 BC), to a numbing awareness that they were now seemingly abandoned and alone in Mesopotamia; from the certainty of their religious rituals centred on the Temple and festivals, to the absence of any commonly accepted religious symbols around them apart from the blatantly pagan ones in Babylon; from confidence in a God who would obviously deliver them, to coming to terms with the fact that God might want to make them once again fit for his purposes by allowing them to become totally vulnerable. What a change of attitude that must have been! And all achieved through exile. We tend to think that we are of most use to God when we are evidently strong, numerous and powerful, but the gospel reminds us that we are at our strongest when at our weakest and so utterly reliant. Indeed the cross, the story of Gideon, the theology of Paul ('My power is made perfect in weakness. Therefore I will boast all the more about my weaknesses, so that Christ's power may rest on me', 2 Corinthians 12.9) all remind us that such weakness is a prerequisite to usefulness.

The attitudes that should be present in the church in this state of exile today are best summed up in the Beatitudes and in the letter sent to the exiles by Jeremiah (Matthew 5.3–12 and Jeremiah 29.1–23). Together they are a manifesto of attitudes for an exiled church. The Beatitudes teach us to cherish spiritual poverty. We are called to poverty of spirit: 'Blessed are the poor in spirit,' said Jesus. Steven Croft, who trained clergy for ministry in Durham, recalls how clergy often admitted to working over 60 hours a week; more than 22 hours were spent in administration compared with 38 minutes a week being spent in prayer. (Address to Portsmouth Diocesan Conference, 'A vision for the Church in the 21st Century'); but often there is little awareness in the Church of England at least that 'you [we] are wretched, pitiful, poor, blind and naked' with a resulting striking dependence on God in prayer (Revelation 3.17, message to the church in Laodicea). Instead there is often pride about our heritage of buildings, history, scholarship and comparative wealth. Again Jesus says, 'Blessed are those who mourn', calling us not only to be compassionate like him towards those who mourn, but also to mourn over our sins and those of our society and world. If on the one hand the Church of England prides itself on its pastoral care offered throughout the country through its public and private ministry, and particularly to those who are bereaved, it should not on the other hand overlook its need to mourn over its own failures and foibles.

Next to be blessed are the meek. The call to be meek is a call to humility and a demonstration of humility is a willingness to listen and change. This means listening to those in parts of the church other than our own, as well as listening to the spiritual search, critique and cry for reality in the lives of those well outside the church but seeking, however clumsily, to know the love and compassion of God. This humility is not only a defence for ourselves but an invitation to others, as Augustine explained.

> Construct no other way for yourself of grasping and holding the truth than the way constructed by Him who, as God, saw how faltering our steps were. This way is first, humility, second, humility, third, humility. And however often you should ask me, I would say the same, not because there are no other precepts to be explained, but if humility does not precede and accompany and follow every good work we do, and if it is not set before us to look upon, and beside us to lean upon, and behind us to fence us in, pride will wrest from our hand any good we do while we are in the very act of taking pleasure in it.
>
> (Augustine, *Sermon* 61.4)

But lest such humility be mistaken for compliance, compromise or toleration of any contrary view or spirit, Jesus then says, 'Blessed are those who hunger and thirst for righteousness, for they shall be satisfied.' Righteousness is a multi-layered word encompassing personal integrity, social justice, the way of peace and God's gift of acceptance. In Matthew the stress is on the endeavour of bringing into being a just and healthy society; in Paul it is receiving the gift of God's justifying righteousness in the context of a new covenant; and for Luke it is the welcome of the outsider into a new and Spirit-directed community. Whoever thirsts for these descriptions of righteousness with a preparedness to change (repentance) will be satisfied or fulfilled. And people who hunger for these things will want them both for themselves and also for others, drawing them into a discipleship that discovers each of these definitions of righteousness.

To achieve this goal will mean being both merciful, as our heavenly Father is merciful, clear in vision or pure in heart as well as being peacemakers, willing to reconcile others wherever possible. So the pursuit of righteousness will inevitably involve the qualities of mercy or compassion, purity and sacrificial peacemaking, just as it did for Jesus himself. And nor is it surprising that such a way of life will quite possibly draw persecution, isolation or misunderstanding. As we have seen, men and women in former generations or centuries have faced such opprobrium and from their exilic stance have called others to a new and more exhilarating, if dangerous, discipleship.

If the Beatitudes form one leg of this manifesto for the contemporary exile then the other leg is supplied by Jeremiah's letter to the exiles in Babylon in the sixth century BC (Jeremiah 29). This letter repays careful study as a word both to that beleaguered community, bewildered by the turn of events they were part of, and also to the church in Britain today seeking its own way forward in a land (society) at once familiar but now strange. The themes of this letter are as follows: the promise of eventual restoration after a definite period of exile (70 years) in Babylon (Jeremiah 29.10); the injunction to the Jewish community to search for God where they were with all their heart and to be content with nothing less (v. 10); the need to build up their own community, both for its own health and as a sign to the surrounding people (v. 6); to take the long view of their time in exile and establish their life there (v. 5); to seek the welfare of the community who had taken them captive, for their welfare is bound up with the exiles' own (v. 7); and, most emphatically, the need not to listen to other voices different from the Prophet's own message, which had been their failure in the past and which was still a temptation in the present, even in exile. In other words, they needed the right understanding as to why they were there and what they should do, it was imperative to hear God aright (v. 8, 9 and v. 19). Now although it would be poor interpretation to make rigid application of a word sent to the exiles in Babylon to a church sensing a new kind of exile in Britain today (especially when it comes to lengths of time or the importance of Jerusalem), nonetheless the principles are highly applicable. The way forward for the church today is to recognize it faces new expressions of Babylon, in whose empire it exists, but nevertheless to work for the welfare of those wittingly or unwittingly marching to that empire's agenda, to pray for and work for its welfare; to seek God and his ways with a whole heart; to build up its own communities as a sign of love, hope and righteousness; to remain faithful, attentive and obedient to his divine word and to keep joyful hope in the promise of eventual vindication and confidence in God's purpose for his people, since he says, then as now, 'I know the plans I have for you, plans for your welfare and not for your harm, to give you a future and a help' (v. 11, NRSV). Taken together this two-fold call, then as now, was not to be a defensive and depressed community of exiles with a siege-mentality waiting for eventual release and escape to a cherished vision of the future: rather it was and is to be an open, generous, hopeful and confident community, becoming a healthy sign of God's presence to an empire that had temporarily captured it but of which it was not a permanent part but where God nevertheless could be found, enjoyed and shared perhaps more effectively than he was in Jerusalem for the previous hundreds of years. And if they grasped it, they had been given reason to be confident by the prophets of their redemption, and of the hope of a New Covenant at the heart of which was restoration and the gift of the Spirit (see Isaiah 53; Ezekiel 36.24–28, ch. 37; Jeremiah 33).

Now that is a picture of what an exiled church in Britain could be like: exiles in an alien empire but free from its pall. So far from the thought of being in exile becoming a deep psychological blow to the mentality or aspirations of the church today, in fact it is the place to hear the extraordinary message of Second Isaiah, not least words like

> But you, Israel, my servant,
>   Jacob, whom I have chosen,
>   the offspring of Abraham my friend;
> you whom I took from the ends of the earth,
>   and called from its farthest corners,
> saying to you, 'You are my servant,

I have chosen you and not cast you off ';
do not fear, for I am with you,
   do not be afraid, for I am your God;
I will strengthen you, I will help you,
   I will uphold you with my victorious right hand.
                                    (Isaiah 41.8–10, NRSV)

So this letter to the exiles from Jeremiah, together with the 'Be-atitudes' of Jesus, gives the church in Britain a tune to which to march, a matrix of attitudes to adopt. The question now is, what kind of spirituality does this engender? What might the resulting spiritual flavour of the church be if someone was to stray into its life? What kind of spirituality would result from these attitudes if they truly took root?

The spirituality of an exiled church

There is probably only an arbitrary dividing line between the attitudes and the spirituality of a church facing increasing exile. Indeed the attitudes, spirituality and manner of mission of the church, as described in the next chapter, are like concentric circles or ripples produced by the stone of reality in the pond of the church's increasing sense of exile in Britain. Our attitudes and spirituality are part of our mission; for people today are more interested in what we *are* than in what we say, and how what we believe in fact affects what we do. Society in general is acutely aware of our world's needs, its injustices and its widespread impoverishment, as well as our planet's dangers, so the question that people are posing explicitly or implicitly is how are Christians facing up to these challenges and what action and hope do they bring?

To describe the kind of spirituality a church facing increasing exile might exhibit is in itself to take on an enormous task in necessarily a brief number of words. In the first instance spirituality is a much overused word and a word which in our pick-and-mix postmodern world can mean what any person wants it to mean. It is therefore an elusive and slippery term that needs a bit of pinning down, especially in a Christian sense. To be valid it must never be divorced from true biblical, orthodox theology (see Smail, 2007, pp. 9ff). Spirituality arises from the dialogue between context and theology. This means, for instance, that although a Christian banker working in a multinational global bank in the City of London and a Sudanese Christian living in Darfur both have hope in the Word made flesh and may have the same basic theology, their spiritualities will be very different. For them 'Give us today our daily bread' will take on quite different meanings. Likewise a church at the start of the twenty-first century, which faces increasing exile, will have a different spirituality from the established state church at the beginning of the twentieth century; again the basic theology is the same but the spirituality is different. The interaction of theology and context results in a cluster of convictions about God, our world and our vocation which determines how we pray, how we understand our calling and how we act both individually and corporately. Whether it realizes it or not, the church in Britain, facing this sense of increasing exile, has begun to use terms which reflect its own self-understanding and spirituality. The words are (and they need to be read slowly) pilgrimage, waiting, lament, transformation, simplicity and generosity or grace; together they form a spirituality which arises from our context and which are rooted in our theology of the hope offered in the Word made flesh. We shall now look at these important words in pairs.

The first pair, which is interrelated, is *pilgrimage* and *waiting*. Talk to any exile, and these two experiences are never far from their consciousness. They are often on a journey and are involved too frequently in interminable waiting. We shall look at each word in turn and their relationship to each other. There can be little doubt that people in general and the church in particular have a heightened sense of being on a pilgrimage or a journey, and this is indicative of both the general search for meaning and transcendence that is present today – indicated perhaps by such TV programmes as *Extreme Pilgrim* or *Earth Pilgrim* – and the more particular sense in the church now of discipleship being a journey or a pilgrimage. Nor is this new: after all, Jesus calls us both to come to him and follow him, and following is all about pilgrimage or journeying; it is dynamic, it is changing and it requires discernment to see where he is going and how we can follow. One of the great classic works of discipleship, *Pilgrim's Progress*, was written by an exile himself, John Bunyan, who chose the prospect of gaol rather than compliance with the state's demands. The difference in this type of spirituality compared to others that have gone before is that it requires a quest to see where we go next both in our mission and in our walk with God; and so instead of simply defending or proclaiming a set of propositional truths we must seek earnestly where and how God is calling us to go now. We are on a journey in which we discover truth along the way and make it known to others. As the Psalmist wrote,

> Blessed are those whose strength is in you,
>   who have set their hearts on pilgrimage.
> As they pass through the Valley of Baca,
>   they make it a place of springs;
>   the autumn rains also cover it with pools.
> They go from strength to strength,
>   till each appears before God in Zion.
>   (Psalm 84.5–7)

If this sense of journey or pilgrimage is heightened in this spirituality for an exiled church then it lays greater weight on both the members and leaders of churches to observe what the next stage of their journey is together. Inevitably this means that leaders and members alike must learn to listen or be attentive to God in waiting upon him.

The Rule of St Benedict (The Prologue and opening sentence) emphasizes the importance of attentive listening as does John of the Cross, who advises that deep prayer is to 'preserve a loving attentiveness to God with no desire to feel or understand any particular thing concerning God' (*Maxims on Love* 9). In other words it is to wait patiently in the presence of God. It is in this context of waiting while on pilgrimage and listening to God that our own pilgrimage is progressed. Like Evagrius, who approached the famous monk Macarius in the Egyptian desert with the request, 'Father, give me a word to live by', and received the response, 'Secure the anchor rope [your mind] to a rock [Christ] and by the grace of God the ship will ride the devilish waves of the beguiling sea', so we approach God himself with the request 'Lord, give me a word to live by!' (see Laird, 2006, p. 37). These words are then food for the journey for, as we know, 'One does not live by bread alone, but by every word that comes from the mouth of God' (Matthew 4.4 and Deuteronomy 8.3, NRSV). Treasuring these words derived from attentive listening and contemplation of Scripture is indeed food for the journey. Again, the common practice today of keeping a spiritual journal reflects the sense that we are on a spiritual journey, a band of exiles making our way to heaven.

The second pair of qualities which should frame the spirituality of an exiled church are the *embrace of lament* and the *hope of transformation*. Once again we turn to Psalm 137 to express the sense of lament. The exiles arrived after their arduous journey from Judah and sat down by the waters of Babylon and wept. And the prophet Ezekiel who accompanied them and lived among them took up these twin motifs of lament and hope throughout his extraordinary prophecy. As Mursell writes, 'Lament might be described as the way you respond when faith and experience collide painfully with one another. It is supremely the prayer of the powerless, of those not in control of what is happening to them' (Mursell, 2005, p. 40). Laments are scattered generously through the Psalms and Prophets and almost always they indicate a sense of exile from God. So the Psalmist cries in Psalm 13,

> How long, O Lord? Will you forget me for ever?
>> How long will you hide your face from me?
> How long must I wrestle with my thoughts
>> and every day have sorrow in my heart?
> How long will my enemy triumph over me?

But by the end the Psalmist has more hope; he says

> But I trust in your unfailing love;
>> my heart rejoices in your salvation.

Or again even before the exile, the prophet Habakkuk, who lived in Judah during the time of its spiritual disintegration, cried out,

> How long, O Lord, must I call for help,
>> but you do not listen?
> Or cry out to you, 'Violence!'
>> but you do not save?
> Why do you make me look at injustice?
>> Why do you tolerate wrong?
> Destruction and violence are before me;
>> there is strife, and conflict abounds.
> Therefore the law is paralysed,
>> and justice never prevails.
>> > (Habakkuk 1.2–4)

But wonderfully by the end of his prophecy Habakkuk was proclaiming,

> Though the fig-tree does not bud
>> and there are no grapes on the vines,

> though the olive crop fails
>> and the fields produce no food,
> though there are no sheep in the pen
>> and no cattle in the stalls,
> yet I will rejoice in the Lord,
>> I will be joyful in God my Saviour.
>
> (3.17–18)

Never was there a clearer case of Brueggemann's perception of the psalms being often divided into a sequence of disorientation and reorientation than in such psalms, or in this pre-exilic prophet.

The point is that a church which feels itself going into exile or is already in exile will express its prayer in a form of lament. Once again this springs from the longing for change in the context of loss. For the Jews in Babylon there was much to lament; the loss of their homeland, their capital city and Temple. For the church in Britain there is no credible lament for its own loss of power or influence, but there is a proper place for a lament for our society and for the failure of the church. We may rightly lament the violence on our streets, the rise of teenage murderers, the absence of care in many homes, the frequent way we break marriage vows, the increasing gap between rich and poor, for a society built on consumerism and debt, without whose excesses recession takes a toll. Here is much ground for lament. At a recent prayer week in our church we put up a tent in a side chapel; it was 'a lamenting tent', a place where people could go and express their own laments: personal, prophetic or social. At root such laments have the anguished prayer of 'How long, Lord?' It seems to me that a church which is true to its calling will express such a lament and invite others in to identify its causes and share its pain, and in that way be drawn into the life of God and his own feelings for us and for our society. But that is only one side of the coin: the other is that it is that such laments are answered by the hope of transformation and with it even the possibility of joy. This may seem utterly contradictory but it is present in the examples from the Psalms and Prophets we have already looked at.

Again Mursell writes,

> We are encountering here perhaps the greatest paradox presented to us by the Bible's reflections on exile: that, while exile remains a deeply destructive experience, God is capable of transforming it

106

into an opportunity for unprecedented envisioning of a new and quite
different future – not only for the exiles but for all creation.

(Mursell, 2005, p. 46)

This surely is the message of Second Isaiah, that amidst their laments
God announces his comfort, and promises to Israel that he will now
do a new thing (Isaiah 40.1 and 43.19) through the Servant whom
he is sending. Likewise Brueggemann wrote,

> Exile did not lead Jews in the Old Testament to abandon faith or
> settle for abdicating despair, nor to retreat to privatised religion. On
> the contrary, exile evoked the most brilliant literature and the most
> daring theological articulation in the Old Testament.
>
> (Brueggemann, 1997, p. 3)

So even alongside the lament there is the hope of transformation; even
in the tent of lament we can put on the habit of hope. This means
celebrating God-given change whether in a person's life, in an act of
transforming love in the wastelands of our cities, or through the hope
given by a single act of kindness. Lament and hope are two sides of
this spirituality which both need to be evident as part of the spirituality of an exiled church.

The last pair of words to describe this spirituality for an exiled church
is *generosity* and *simplicity*. Together with the other parts of this six-
sided paradigm they complete a kind of trellis upon which the life
of the church can grow both attractively and hopefully. The pattern
for the kind of generosity we are thinking of here comes from the
generosity of God himself, for that is the true basis of all generosity,
both its inspiration and its guide. All our generosity begins with
receiving God's generosity to us, as Paul says: 'Thanks be to God for
his indescribable gift!' (2 Corinthians 9.15). Elsewhere Paul cannot
find enough superlatives to describe this indescribable gift; so in
Ephesians he writes of the riches of God's grace that 'he lavished upon
us with all wisdom and understanding' (1.8) or 'the riches of his
glorious inheritance' (1.18) which we are to know, or the 'love that
surpasses knowledge' (3.19) which we are to grasp with a 'knowing'
that is at the same time inadequate for the task. The point is that the
church itself can be generous only when it has grasped the generosity that God has made known to it in Christ. And so the meanness of
our church life is often a reflection of our inadequate comprehension
of the Father's generosity. True generosity, lavish grace, begins with

God and must be received with faith, gratitude and joy. As Miroslav Volf writes in his Lent book of 2006, 'God's love does not suck out the good it finds in others, as distorted human love does. "It flows forth and bestows good"' (Volf, 2006, p. 49 quoting Luther, 1959, p. 57). Yes, generosity rightly received flows forth and bestows good.

The church in Britain is waking up to the fact that its resources are not money in the bank, real estate, or historic buildings, all of which have their drawbacks, but the receipt of the unmerited generosity of God. It is this that enables the thought of bestowing, without expectation of return, 'a million acts of kindness' (the strapline of a inter-church movement called Hope '08), encouraging local churches to give away food, gifts, or precious time to improve the look of our estates and high streets, and to do so as the outworking of being recipients of indescribable generosity ourselves. It is this that made an Anglican clergyman, Chris Woods, say to his impoverished congregation in St Helen's, Lancashire, when the collection was announced: 'If anyone needs to, please help yourselves as the collection is passed round' (Obituary, *Telegraph*, 16 January 2008). And, of course, all these gestures of generosity are merely preludes to making known God's own indescribable gift which is Christ himself. So the experience and sharing of generosity, with celebration, is very much part of the spirituality of a church in exile.

The final side of our spirituality for an exiled church is simplicity. Simplicity is not the same as being simpletons, in just the same way that childlikeness is not the same as childishness. Jesus, once asked by the disciples for an example of greatness, did not point to the rabbinic teachers in Israel but called a child with all its simplicity into their midst and said, 'I tell you the truth, unless you change and become like little children, you will never enter the kingdom of heaven. Therefore, whoever humbles himself like this child is the greatest in the kingdom of heaven' (Matthew 18.1–4). The simplicity of a child is defined by both trust and innocence: likewise the church is to be simple in its trust and pure in its innocence. Nor is innocence the same as being naive about corruption or evil, for again we are called 'to be innocent as doves and wise as serpents'. This combination will define our simplicity. Simplicity is further defined by sincere thought, which is able to reduce things to their essentials, not necessarily by acquiring more and more knowledge, but by intuitive and Spirit-led reflection. Simplicity is about seeing the needful thing and pursuing it single-mindedly. Once again the monastic tradition can help us here. Benedict accepted the value of material things and their use in enhancing life, but they were regarded still with detachment (de Waal, 1999, p. 85). Likewise Charles Wesley made this abundantly clear in the words of his hymn 'Forth in thy name, O Lord I go':

> The task thy wisdom hath assigned
> O let me cheerfully fulfil:
> In all my works thy presence find,
> And prove thy good and perfect will.

In other words it is the simplicity of finding God and living for God in the 'ordinary' which is at the heart of this kind of spirituality, something which was made plain by Brother Lawrence years ago, but which we would do well to rediscover. Nor can we live in our world with its threat of global warming resulting from long years of dependence on cheap carbon fossil fuels and our profligate waste of materials in our throw-away Western society without committing to a lifestyle which takes care of our planet. At the heart of this living will be simplicity, and the trick will be for both governments and individuals alike to provide fulfilment and satisfaction in work and leisure which are not so carbon-energy dependent. Surely this is a call to a simplicity that takes account of being responsible stewards. And which community is better placed to take leadership in it than the church? After all, our founder has called us to simplicity – he it was who carefully gathered up the fragments at the end of the feeding of the five thousand. We are to be decoupled from a materialist lifestyle and given different spiritual and moral aspirations in the context of being stewards of creation, and in particular of that small or large part of it for which we have responsibility, whether window box or large estate. Nor does this necessarily mean a hair-shirt approach to our material existence, but it does mean combining a generous and a simple lifestyle when it comes to material welfare.

These six ideas will, to a large but not exclusive extent, define the spirituality of a church in exile. But it goes almost without saying that they are bound together by a love for God and love of neighbour that is the true starting point of all Christian spirituality. Today more than ever we are called to know that we are pilgrims on a spiritual journey, often waiting patiently and with longing for the fulfilment of the Kingdom; we lament our own failures that have brought us to this point, and those of the society of which we are a part, but nevertheless we hope in the power of God's transforming grace. And finally we act generously as God has lavished his generosity on us in Christ, and we commit ourselves to living simply.

This spirituality, together with the earlier mentioned attitudes found in the Beatitudes and Jeremiah's great letter of hope to the exiles in Babylon, defines the attitudes and spirituality of a church in exile. They are also the essential bedrock to and partner of the mission of a church in exile, to which we must finally turn.

7

The way of mission for an exiled church

Anyone joining a new family, perhaps as a daughter or son-in-law, will be conscious of at least two sets of common interlocking values operating within this one community: one set determining the family's way of relating together (their spirituality, if you like), and another set relating to their preferred activities and their relationship with the outside world (their mission). These twin sets of values will feed off each other and will at times be hard to divide. Indeed the way they take part in their 'mission activities' (cycling, travelling, camping, etc.) will be affected by their spirituality (the way they relate to each other) and equally their spirituality will be shaped by their mission. The differences in dynamic, rather than confessional terms, between family and church are slight, but it is as certain that the church exists by mission as that a fire exists by burning (Emil Brunner), whereas although a family might well become stale without such 'mission' activities, its very existence would not be threatened. And as Archbishop Temple famously and enduringly said, and I paraphrase, the church is the only organization which exists for those who are not yet its members. Of course its mission of making Jesus Christ known through the gospel, with which it has been entrusted, is the Father's mission which he works through the church. For he it was who originally 'so loved the world that he gave his only Son' (John 3.16), and that giving is at the heart of mission.

What we have observed, especially in the more historical section of this book, is that the church has gone about God's mission in remarkably different ways, more different even than the New Testament authors envisaged or recorded in their writings. David Bosch in his classic work on Mission (Bosch, 1991) charts the same paradigm shifts in mission as Küng does in his history of the church. Each mission paradigm in history is noted by Bosch for its different emphasis. Thus

111

the Greek church made the church not the instrument of mission but the goal of it (Bosch, 1991, p. 207); the Roman medieval church required submission to the papacy as the basis of inclusion in the saved community, force being used if necessary; the Protestant church made submission to the Word through faithful obedience its central tenet of mission and the effect of the Enlightenment on mission especially among the Protestant churches was to open the door to individualism so that the community of the church became less important than the convictions of the individual. But the mission of God conducted through the church had to change, not in its message but in the way it was expressed. With the great change in Western culture and the paradigm shift which took place from the 1960s onwards, the expression of the gospel and the style of mission had to change equally in order to meet the new situation. Whereas previously a 'come to us' rather than a 'go to them' dynamic existed alongside a presumption that people had a familiarity with Christian language and the Christian story, no such things can now be taken for granted. Indeed more recently questions have been asked about what exactly church 'is'. Need it be a meeting lasting for an hour or so and consisting of long singing, long listening and long liturgy? Is this what Jesus envisaged? When is church 'church', and what truly constitutes mission? We are at a place where, rather like disassembling a rusty old car, we are asking which bits of its worn out engine and chassis we should keep to use in a new model that is capable of modern travel, and which bits should be discarded? Indeed, does it all need to be scrapped and a new assembly line made to construct a purpose-built model for this generation's needs? And, of course, the church operates in the real world where there isn't always the option of converting old church buildings, which may even require special planning permission, into more user-friendly environments. And indeed, church life is not about finding uses for buildings but about growing communities of faith in God and love for him and neighbour. Blue-sky thinking may be possible, but blue-sky action in our constrained and regulated environment is more difficult and is quite another matter. The fact is that in Britain in what is called a post-Christian society we are only too aware that, as Joshua said to the Israelites who were entering the Promised Land, 'You have never been this way before' (Joshua 3.4). We are also on a virgin journey – in a landscape which is familiar, with literally spires and church towers every few miles, but in quite a different culture that demands quite a different missionary approach. Indeed we have not 'been this way before', and so what follows are some principles of mission for an exiled church to guide us forward on this journey.

Incarnational mission

The final and concluding act of God's mission to the world began with the incarnation. Previously he had chosen a people, the Jews; then he had sent them the prophets and then he sent them his Son. God's mission was always about sending his representatives of increasing seniority until he came himself. This was encapsulated in Jesus own parable of the tenants (Matthew 21.33–46), in which God came himself to his unruly tenants. This truth marks Christianity out from all other religions: in no other religion did God offer himself in redeeming sacrifice for his unruly world. And unruly it is; as Bertrand Russell famously said, the world resembles a lunatic asylum in which the inmates have taken control and the key has been thrown away! Thankfully in the incarnation God found a way of re-entering his world in person and was bent on redeeming what he found. Incarnation or 'becoming human' was at the heart of Jesus' mission. Without the incarnation there was no possibility of redemption, no vision of a fully human life and no hope of resurrection. Everything is predicated on the incarnation as Athanasius so powerfully argued in *de Incarnatione* in refuting Arius. God really did come in flesh: fully God and fully man. And in coming, he made himself utterly vulnerable, the mark of which was his eventual rejection. 'He came to that which was his own, but his own did not receive him' (John 1.11). In other words, for Jesus, mission involved complete commitment and utter vulnerability to those to whom he had come. Likewise the church today can no longer come on its own terms, as it did in the days of Christendom, to the population at large but rather it must come with humility offering loving service, with a message that both inspires and pervades its action, to a world that is intrigued, has echoes of the Christian past in its collective mind (which too can often be unhelpful) but has largely turned its back on church if not Jesus.

The principle of incarnation must, more than any other, be the guiding star of the mission of the exiled church. No longer can the church corral or constrain its own members, let alone those outside its community; instead, only attractive and self-evident life will attract people. In their book *The Shaping of Things to Come* Frost and Hirsch tell how farmers gather their sheep in the Australian outback. Whereas in Britain, except in some hill farming, animals are for the most part contained by walls or fences, this is impossible in the vast areas of the outback. Instead there the only way of attracting and keeping flocks or herds is by sinking wells – the animals will voluntarily stay near to drinking water. A well in their midst is the answer to both attracting and keeping the flock together (Frost and Hirsch, 2007, pp. 47, 48). Nor is it surprising that in Second Isaiah God continually refers to the provision of water, a picture of spiritual refreshment, as the prerequisite for renewed spiritual life. So Isaiah prophesies,

> 'Forget the former things;
>   do not dwell on the past.
> See, I am doing a new thing!
>   Now it springs up; do you not perceive it?
> I am making a way in the desert
>   and streams in the wasteland.'
> (Isaiah 43.18–19)

The provision of attractive and refreshing salvation lay at the heart of the new thing that God was doing. The church in its mission needs to find ways to become a self-evident place of refreshment and transformation in a culture desperate for truly thirst-quenching spirituality.

For the church's mission to be incarnational means that it might well take on tasks of loving service for the community. Just as the church in second-century Rome took on the task of caring for the 1,500 widows – looked after by 46 presbyters and 14 deacons and sub-deacons (H. Chadwick, 1993, p. 56) – so loving and appropriate service to the community, or some part of it, with no strings attached, is a further step in the incarnating of Jesus today. So projects that provide food, clothing and furniture free of any charge to those who are homeless or who are setting up home in newly provided accommodation through Christian organizations such as Genesis in Bath (which uses around 300 volunteers to feed the homeless) or the Besom in London and elsewhere, continue an incarnational ministry, making known God's love in tangible and practical ways. It is then that some of the deep searches in people's hearts can be met.

There are commonly thought to be four great searches that pervade our modern society; the searches for transcendence, meaning (or significance), community and intimacy. The mission of the church is in part to show how Jesus is the ultimate answer to each one of these, but it cannot begin this task if it is hidden away, behind its walls, singing its songs, listening to its sermons and barely visible to its local community. Incarnation is about coming down, coming out and becoming vulnerable, which surely is the first step in mission. It was for Jesus. Nothing could have been achieved if he hadn't come. 'The incarnation demands that we neither retreat into a holier-than-thou Christian ghetto nor give ourselves over to the values of secular culture. And let's be honest this is the most dangerous place of all' (Frost, 2006, p. 15). So mission begins as it always has with a preparedness to become incarnate, visible, audible and tangible (see 1 John 1.1–4) in our world. Paradoxically, a church in exile is not to hide away but begin once more on the same path of becoming incarnate in cultures it must observe, study and respond to. The next step in this process is that the church must become contextual.

Contextual mission

The simple truth is that since we have left the world of Christendom behind, a church which holds on to a model of ministry designed for that age will soon find itself out of touch with the bulk of the population. Is this one of the reasons why the Church of England mostly has a membership of over 50 years old, except in those 'minister' churches (i.e. a church with greater resources than a normal parish church and with a wider ministry than simply its own parish) which are able to afford multifaceted ministry to attract a much wider age range? Contextual mission means responding to the culture from which the church is trying to attract new members. Indeed,

> Contextualisation can be defined as the dynamic process whereby the constant message of the gospel interacts with specific, relative situations . . . Contextualisation attempts to communicate the gospel in word and deed and to establish churches in ways that make sense to people within their cultural context. (Frost and Hirsch, 2007, p. 83)

Or in other words the communication of the gospel should offend for the right and not the wrong reasons. If a church persists in keeping a model of church which is far removed from the culture of its host community or from the network of people with a similar culture that it is seeking to reach, then it will simply fail to communicate with the people in those cultures and so fail in its missionary objective. In that case it will have retreated into a kind of self-imposed exile rather than being an exilic community seeking to draw into its fellowship those who are attracted by its message and life. In other words all Christians in Britain are now involved in cross-cultural mission and we need to learn from the mistakes and successes of other cross cultural missionaries who went in former years to South America, Asia and Africa.

A review of the missionary movements in these continents is beyond the scope of this short book. However, what we do know is that when missionary movements, with undeniable courage and sacrifice still honoured in the countries they went to, arrived in those countries they brought not only the gospel but also forms of worship more suited to (say) either Tractarian worship in Oxford or Roman Catholic worship in central Italy. The buildings they built resembled the parish churches and cathedrals of the West, the vestments they wore were hardly suited to the tropics and the hymns that were sung were little related to the rhythms and expressions of, for example, the Africans. But to go there today, for Anglicans at least, is to see Anglican worship both more faithful to its tradition and more vibrant in its expression than can be found in Britain; part of the reason for this may be that the host cultures are more receptive now in Africa than they are in the West from where these models originated. It is an interesting thought. Nonetheless, despite this assimilation of some defining characteristics of Anglicanism in Africa and its evident success there, the underlying principle of contextualizing the gospel must still be taken forward. For if that process of contextualization does not take place, then discipleship in such churches may prove to be only skin deep.

One of the greatest examples of contextualization in a missionary context is that of Vincent Donovan, written up in his *Christianity Rediscovered*. A Roman Catholic missionary, Donovan decided to jettison all the accretions of Western missionary models, with their dependence on education and medicine as attractional lures and, instead, simply to go and talk to the Masai people in Southern Kenya about Jesus and what he had come to do. He wrote movingly, I think, to his bishop in May 1966 as follows:

> As of this month, in the seventh year of this mission's existence, there are no adult Masai practising Christians from Loliondo mission. The only practising Christians are the catechist and the hospital medical dresser, who have come here from other sections of Masailand . . . I suddenly feel the urgent need to cast aside all theories and discussions, all efforts and strategy and simply go to these people and do the work among them for which I came to Africa.

He went on:

> I would propose cutting myself off from the schools and the hospital as far as these people are concerned – as well as socialising with them – and just talk to them about God and the Christian message. I know this is a *radical* [my italics] departure from traditional procedure, but the very fact that it be considered so shows the state we are in. (Donovan, 2005, p. 13)

And so began a moving and remarkable experiment in mission. The Masai God was Engai and now, like Paul in Athens, Donovan made known to them the God whom they long suspected to exist, but whom they did not truly know. Donovan gave flesh to their idea of God which was formed by their land, their cattle, their struggles and their view of the world and in their language which lacked a future tense. Of Jesus, Donovan said:

> This is the news I bring to you. The word has gone out over all the earth, and I believe it, that in the man Jesus, from the town of Nazareth in the country of the Jews, God has told us what he is like, has shown us who and what he is. The word is that Jesus is the answer to your questions and mine. For a few short years, which seem like only a few seconds in the life of any man or any people, Jesus pulled aside the dark heavy clouds that hide God from us, and for one, brief shining moment showed us a glimpse of God, showed us what God is, and what he is like, what he feels. (Donovan, 2005, p. 56)

Here Donovan encultured or contextualized the Christian message in the most basic element of their culture, their language. He went to the host culture abandoning his own, living among them simply, and communicating the message in their language and in their ideas.

way

This surely echoes what Jesus did. The missionary trick is to remain faithful to the message, not emptying it of its power or truth but making the message and life known in the host culture to which it goes. Another example among many in Britain is in Polzeath, Cornwall. The culture in which the church is seeking to operate is the surfing community of North Cornwall, and the church is called the Tubestation, referring to 'the tube' so beloved of surfers in which the most exciting rides may be found. The language it uses is for the surfer. It is another example of contextualizing the gospel. A church that has long since been beached by the Christendom tide and left naked on the shoreline cannot put back on the same old clothes. It must adapt to a new milieu and present its message in different ways to different cultures. Its exile from the old Christendom culture is a wake-up call to go back to its roots and express itself in new, innovative and imaginative ways. It is therefore time, as Donovan, said to be radical.

Radical mission

The word 'radical' is much overused (and misused). It literally means 'going back to roots', *radix* being 'root' in Latin. In the context of Christian mission this surely means going back to Jesus: his life, teaching, style and manner. In an important sentence about mission today, Frost and Hirsch write, 'An incarnational ministry draws not-yet-Christians toward God by exciting curiosity through storytelling, by provoking a sense of wonder and awe, by showing extraordinary love, by exploring how God has touched our lives, and by focussing on Jesus' (Frost and Hirsch, 2007, p. 112). This is what Donovan did when he went to the Masai seeking to explain the coming of Jesus in their language, using their terms and on their territory, but at the same time telling the unique story of Jesus as described in the Bible. So to be radical is to return to the unvarnished truth of Jesus' life, ministry, death and resurrection, explaining its significance for all people in a way which answers, ideally, questions already provoked by the lifestyle of the Christian community (see Tomlin, 2002). And we should do this conscious that we are exiles in the culture we live in.

When the Jews arrived in Babylon as exiles they too needed to rediscover their roots before they could once again bear an authentic witness to the God who had called them through Abraham centuries before. When they first arrived by the waters of Babylon they must have looked a dispirited, downcast, bedraggled lot quite unable to respond to the taunts of their captors with anything other than a shrug. 'Sing us one of the Lord's songs,' their captors taunted. In response they sat down and wept. Their situation was desperate and perplexing. How had they come to be there? What had happened? Their Temple was destroyed, their city brutally smashed, their society smitten and their communities scattered. Heart-searching was not in it: they plumbed the depths of their souls for answers. To understand, God must speak, and he did through his servants the prophets. It was to be a time of rediscovery and no one was more important in this than Isaiah who reassured them of God's faithfulness to them.

> 'But you, O Israel, my servant,
>   Jacob, whom I have chosen,
>   you descendants of Abraham my friend,
> I took you from the ends of the earth,
>   from its farthest corners I called you.
> I said, "You are my servant";
>   I have chosen you and have not rejected you.
> So do not fear, for I am with you;
>   do not be dismayed, for I am your God.
> I will strengthen you and help you;
>   I will uphold you with my righteous right hand.'
>   (Isaiah 41.8–10)

In other words, the Israelites were taken back to the root of their calling. There was nothing that commended them to God in and of themselves (see Deuteronomy 4 especially), but rather God's own choice of Abraham and his descendants by whom all the world would be blessed through that other descendant of Abraham, Jesus.

So while in exile the Jews were taken back to the root of their calling, which did not depend on the Temple or even the Law (the Torah), but on God's own faithful and sovereign choice to which he remained committed. And since this God 'reigned' over all the earth (see Isaiah 52.7–10) and all the nations were to him like a drop in the ocean, then seeking him would work out for their deliverance as was promised beforehand (see Deuteronomy 4.25ff – a very important passage), provided they sought him with all their heart. So exile brought about a renewed seeking of God, a return to the root of their vocation and, with that, renewed hopes for the future since God was sovereign, and reigned both then and now.

Without wanting to draw too exact parallels between the church today and the exile in Babylon, might there nevertheless be lessons for today? Is there not a call to a radical return to our own vocation, living in the context as we do of other empires, and to follow the command of another Prophet, this time Micah, who summarized our calling: 'What does the Lord require of you? To act justly and to love mercy and to walk humbly with your God' (Micah 6.8). To be radical is to return to our most basic calling, to rediscover the root of our faith, to focus on Jesus in a way fitting for our times.

The second way in which we are called to be radical is to simply present Jesus (rather than Christianity) in a way which invites participation rather than confrontation. In *Preaching to Exiles*, Walter Brueggeman's important book on this theme, he argues that our preaching in the context of ourselves being exiles in the midst of other empires should not be monolithic, bludgeoning or over-systematic, but rather allow 'space, room for manoeuvre, breathing opportunities that allow for negotiation, adjudication, ambiguity and playfulness' in the response of the listener. In other words, just as Jesus' teaching to the crowds was always in parables (see Mark 4.34), so our preaching might at times be oblique, inviting curiosity rather than leaving little to the imagination. We need to whisper to people's souls rather than initially confront their wills. Whispering to souls involves sharing our vulnerabilities as well as our certainties; it means at first telling the stories of Jesus' life more than explaining the doctrines that underlie them; it means allowing time for response to develop rather than pushing for decisions; it needs to engage with imagination through art whether drama, films, music and poetry, rather than putting it all out there.

One fine example of this type of communication comes from breaking in Mustang horses as recorded by Monty Roberts in his book called *The Man who Listens to Horses* (similar to the blockbuster novel and film *The Horse Whisperer*). Roberts discovered something very interesting when observing Mustangs in the wild; when they become separated from the herd they become sick and even die. Using this insight and applying it to the breaking in of these wild horses, he decided that when breaking them in in the ring he would neither make eye contact with them, nor even approach them, on the theory that they craved relationships even with their enemy more than being ignored and left alone. Amazingly, in this way it was possible to put a saddle on them, and even a rider after one hour, rather than enduring days of confrontation and struggle until the horse was exhausted and submissive and its will was broken (Roberts, 1997, p. 98). Likewise there is a place for whispering the good news of the gospel today through the experience of a loving community, through exposure to the beauty of creation and the affirmation of agape-love, through Christians' stories of God's intervention in their lives and through arousing interest in what makes a Christian tick and thereby provoking, hopefully, questions whose answer is truly listened to. Whispering to the soul of others must become part of the appeal of the church in exile and it is no more or less than the way God treated his servants. After all, when Elijah waited at the mouth of his cave on Horeb for God's answer to his lament, we are told that God was not in the wind, the earthquake or the fire but in 'a gentle whisper' (1 Kings 19.13). If God chose to speak in a whisper, then there is no need for us to think that the only way people hear is through a megaphone. So to be radical is to be unashamed in our focus on Jesus and to speak of him in such a way that others may listen; and in doing this we are far more likely to be truly spiritual.

Spiritual mission

The word 'spiritual' like its sister word 'spirituality' can be a slippery one, capable in our world of almost any interpretation. At its root there is the recognition that as humans we are spiritual beings; that we are body, soul and spirit as well as heart, mind and strength. The extraordinary vitality of our life revolves around the interplay of those six axes. One of the unforeseen phenomena in recent years is that far from the scientific or materialist explanation of life sweeping the board as we thought it might in the 1980s, it has proved inadequate and unsatisfying in providing an explanation for living and for life. Even in Russia, where Stalinist communism sought the end of Christianity, the Orthodox Church has gone through something of a revival even if in part through restoration of an age-old reassociation of church and state.

The rise in our culture of interest in the metaphysical, the magical and the spiritual is for all to see: the success of J. K. Rowling, the novels of Philip Pullman, the interest in J. R. R. Tolkien and *The Lord of the Rings* are testimony to the prevailing interest in a spiritual if not always a Christian explanation of life. For this reason, that is, the general revival of interest in spirituality and a metaphysical explanation of life, we can expect that the more aggressive attacks of secularists like Dawkins, although polemical and temporarily bestselling, will probably have a short shelf life. Quite apart from the fact that many scientists find Dawkins' science suspect, there have been others before him who have proclaimed the end of God, like Voltaire in the eighteenth century, and here we are two hundred years on discussing the same issues with a vastly increased global Christian population. No, what seems irrepressible is the metaphysical or spiritual quest in humans; for no sooner has some humanly devised theory sought to put a lid on this spiritual quest – whether it is Marxism, scientific materialism or indeed Chinese state-capitalism/communism – than this innate spiritual quest either displaces the lid, springs up underground or simply grows up elsewhere.

What is quite clear in our own culture is that there is both a widespread lack of interest in organized or institutional religion and an equally widespread yearning for a spiritual explanation of life. Nor is it quite as simple as that: often the yearning for spiritual things finds deep expression in ancient places of prayer like cathedrals, which are the very embodiment of the institutional church. Indeed in a recent telephone poll of 1002 adults in the UK, 85 per cent said they had been in a church building in the previous year, for a host of reasons (*Church Times*, 1 February 2008). Perhaps all that can be said is that this spiritual quest is, as with so much in our postmodern world, a pick-and-mix thing, and that people's spiritual expression or starting points will be as varied as soaking up the atmosphere of ancient places of prayer or listening to Rachmaninov's Vespers surrounded by candles while in the bath! Once again the task of the church and its mission is, in the words of an Anglican prayer, to show that only in Jesus can all our hungers be satisfied, and to affirm the reality of each individual's spiritual quest (Eucharistic Prayer G: *Common Worship*).

If this is the kind of spiritual milieu in which we find ourselves and in which there is today a strong, if sometimes misdirected, spiritual search, then once again we can learn from the experience of the Jewish exiles. Whereas before the exile the Jews had lived in their own Jewish-dom (as opposed to Christendom) with the institutions of monarchy and Temple to look to (like Christendom, quite often wrongly) now in Babylon they were in a foreign empire and all those institutions had been removed. There was no king, no Temple, no familiar land to give order to their lives by its recurring seasonal demands and its rhythm of festivals. What they came to rely on was a combination of God's prophetic word, especially through Jeremiah, Second Isaiah and Ezekiel, their own prayers and the example of courageous Jews like Daniel and Esther dealing with the power of the empire and bearing a testimony to the universality of their God. God was not bound to Temple, monarchy and land, even if they were; and it was time for them to understand this even at the cost of being removed forcibly from their own land. Likewise, whereas during Christendom the church in Britain could rely on being a national institution, with its power and status in the land, the guardian of the nation's moral consensus, now it finds itself an exilic community being reshaped by the Word of God, responsive to God's prophetic word, led by the Spirit, more dependent on prayer and the testimony of its members in dealing with the empires that confront it. And, not surprisingly, this form of spirituality may well be more compelling than the kind it replaces.

The ingredients of an authentic spiritual life which will resonate with onlookers of this exilic community is a way of life that has integrity, no longer drawing a false boundary between the sacred and the secular, thus doing away with the false dualism that has dogged the church for so long. The dualism that divides faith from the everyday or the ordinary seems rightly phoney to the onlooker. No, if God is worshipped, he must be as much worshipped in the home as in the church, in business as in Bible study, on the beach as in the bedroom. In other words, a Christian's spiritual life must be truly authentic throughout and not a show for specifically religious occasions. It should show itself to be a genuine progress towards becoming fully human (see Whitworth, 2003), in which both our humanity and our diversity are celebrated, and our individuality affirmed and nurtured. In this context we should be able to be entirely honest about our hopes and aspirations, our failures and disappointments, and if necessary to live uncomfortably with paradoxes and unanswered questions rather than seeking to show that we know the answers, because often we truly don't. In other words, an authentic spiritual journey is one that is truly honest about our limitations but nevertheless truly hopeful that God by his Spirit is graciously transforming us, despite our many weaknesses and failures. Such a spiritual life cannot take place except in community to which we must now turn.

Communal mission

Once again we are in the realms of an overused, if nonetheless a vital, word. There is no doubt that 'community', in terms of a safe and inclusive group of people in which there is trust and mutual support, has been greatly eroded in Western society, including in Britain, over the past forty years. This has been the result of a number of social trends. People who are old enough to remember the pre-war days in Britain or life in the 1950s will remember the sense of community that existed in the terraced houses of our cities or in the villages. Doors were left unlocked or even open, children would play in the streets, parents would rub along together, fathers and mothers would work nearby in industries which employed large numbers of local people and often holidays would be taken at home or away in the same weeks of the year. All this would make for community. But now, when I worked on a South London housing estate in the 1990s, few people would open front doors and many would speak through their letter-boxes. There is no denying the poverty and prejudice that existed in pre- and immediately post-war days, but fear and suspicion in our communities seems to have increased. Children are often socially isolated, spending hours on their own in front of TVs or computers, often in their own bedrooms. Many people have no knowledge of their neighbours – some even die and are not discovered for days. (In Bristol recently a man was tragically not discovered until eight years after he died.) What sociologists call 'social capital' is fast being used up in an upsurge of anxiety and suspicion. In her book *Journeying Out* Ann Morisy describes how a young mother with a child, an infant and a buggy wishes to descend a staircase on the Tube but can only do so with the help of others. Such is the climate of suspicion and fear that the mother is anxious about enlisting help from passing fellow travellers, and likewise the fellow travellers, especially the men, are wary about giving help, because they are thinking of the child protection laws. She concludes, 'The bad news is that . . . day-to-day attentiveness to the needs of others is in sharp decline' (Morisy, 2004, pp. 45, 46). The result, social capital – neighbour helping neighbour – is diminished and a sense of community is further reduced.

In an overall situation in which the local community has been undermined by everything from the motor car to the supermarket, one of the greatest strengths the church has to offer is community. But community is really only produced by common shared experiences and in the context of deep acceptance. Community is not produced by self-consciously seeking to make it; rather it is created by an element of shared experience, both spiritual and practical, in which people become dependent on each other and share a sense of danger or risk; in which there is a tangible sense of love and trust. Michael Frost makes the distinction in *Exiles* between community and *communitas*. The latter is not a club, self-interested, inward-looking and safe but rather a group that is task-focused, engaged in something risky (mission), liminal and on the edge, and truly dependent on each other (Frost, 2006, p. 111). The institutional church in Britain has often been a community in the sense of a club; and in more comfortable areas of the UK this is still a real danger: church members are so taken up with sustaining their own church life, that they become insulated from their communities and consequently hard to enter. The best judge of whether a particular church is a community is the outsider or newcomer who comes to one or other aspect of its life, and finds something attractive, welcoming and meaningful.

There is no doubt that a vital part of Jesus' ministry was the formation of a new community. It had at its centre both a new covenant, in which there was forgiveness of sins, as well as a new commandment, which was to love each other. Its central theme was the Kingdom of God (see Whitworth, 2006), and its missional task was the making known of this Kingdom through acts of loving service. This community was in a continual state of movement; in Jesus' case this community of disciples was literally moving around the Judean countryside, and at times going outside it to Samaria or the Decapolis. It was sustained by times of withdrawal and rest, a counterweight to those times when there was hardly time to eat. Meals themselves formed an important part of their life together whether provided by friends like Lazarus and his sisters, sinners like Levi or members of the religious establishment like Simon. Likewise within our churches there must be what Steven Croft has called 'transforming communities', groups of varying size where people can belong and where there is

> depth of friendship and relationship; discipleship within structures of mutual accountability; worship and prayer which arise from and are closely related to shared lives; and a common sense of persons enabling one another to share in the mission of God.
>
> (Croft, 2002, p. 72)

They will be transforming in two ways if working healthily: transforming their own members 'from one degree of glory to another' (2 Corinthians 5.18), but also to some degree providing a measure of transformation in the wider communities they are a part of. Indeed Alasdair MacIntyre in his perceptive book *After Virtue*, having applauded the monastic movement in the early Middle Ages for sustaining civility, virtue and morality in the Dark Ages in their communities, concludes that for our times,

> What matters at this stage is the construction of local forms of community within which civility and the intellectual and moral life can be sustained through the new dark ages which are already upon us. This time the barbarians are not waiting beyond the frontier; they have been governing us for some time. And it is our lack of consciousness of this that constitutes part of our predicament. We are waiting not for Godot, but for another – doubtless very different – St Benedict.
>
> (MacIntyre, 1981, p. 245)

Building communities is vital to our missional effectiveness and the key element of their life is the relationships and friendships that sustain them.

Relational mission

The building block of church life is its relationships. They are to be windows into the working of the gospel; a gospel of grace looking for faith, a gospel of change demanding commitment. As Newbigin so rightly observed, the only hermeneutic of the gospel is a community which believes and lives by it. As we have already said, too often the church or its members have proclaimed that they believe the doctrines of the faith but dualism (the separation of belief from action) has infected our lives so that there is too little evidence of its making much difference to our everyday life. We have been guilty of a reality failure in which we readily sing, 'They will know we are Christians by our love', but then provide precious little evidence to encourage their belief! No, what is inescapable is that our relationships and the conduct of them are a window on the gospel.

There is a widespread desire in our broken lives of twenty-first-century Britain for stable, meaningful and close relationships. Indeed, the search for intimacy is one of the deep and defining quests of our age, along with quests for significance, transcendence and community, all of which the church must attend to. In her book *The Search for Intimacy*, Elaine Storkey writes that 'in our contemporary culture there is a deep and widespread longing for close relationships' (Storkey, 1995, p. 12). It is exacerbated by the all-too-common fracturing of relationships in our society, with high divorce rates and much alienation or neglect between teenagers and parents. The growth of knife and gun crime on our streets among the teenage community, as well as more frequent unprovoked attacks of appalling violence on people (for example the gang of youths who in 2007 attacked and killed Gary Newlove when he intervened to prevent antisocial behaviour outside his home in Cheshire) is no doubt partly the result of broken relationships at home. So there is a frightening breakdown of relationships, while there is a deep yearning for intimacy, often lived out vicariously through celebrity culture or soaps, in which we seem to know the stars of the screen or stage (whether Amy Winehouse or Britney Spears) and their failures, successes and foibles better than we do members of our own family. Here is an irony: a deep fracturing of relationships and a deep longing for friendship at one and the same time. 'What is unique about the present time is that humanity has never been so conscious of the primacy of its intimate concerns, nor expressed them so openly, in almost every part of the globe' (Zeldin, 1995, p. 470).

The church may be in a kind of exile in Britain today but we have nevertheless been given the key to understanding and sustaining relationships. In a recent DVD series produced by Peter Price, Bishop of Bath and Wells, he outlines the conduct of our relationships as follows:

You show wisdom by trusting people
You handle leadership by serving
You handle offenders by forgiving
You handle money by sharing
You handle enemies by loving
You handle violence by suffering.
(see *Changing Lives for Good*, six-part DVD: Bath and Wells
Diocesan Board of Finance 2007)

The challenge will be to conduct our relationships in that way so
that someone stumbling into our hopefully changing communities
will see a different way of conducting life and through that an attractive God. After all, God has committed himself to working both through
the church and thankfully well beyond the church in his mission of
drawing all people to his Son. So, last, a church facing exile in our
society needs to be intentionally missional.

A mission-focused church

The church must be directed by and equipped for mission. A church
which is in a kind of exile must not become self-serving, defensive
and inward-looking. For it to be missional means it must truly exist
for others who are not yet Christians, and for a world burdened with
either exploitation or injustice. Just as the exiles in Babylon needed
to revive their vocation to be a light for the nations, and no longer
to be an exclusive community which regarded others with at best
suspicion and at worst outright hostility, so the church today needs
to be confident of its vocation and humble in its loving attention
to a confused and broken humanity. In his great work *Transforming
Mission*, David Bosch (who incidentally largely follows the same
paradigm shifts as Küng) quotes Moltmann who wrote, 'It is not
the church that has a mission of salvation to fulfil in the world, it
is the mission of the Son and the Spirit through the Father that
includes the church' (Moltmann, 1977, p. 64). And as Bosch goes
on to explain, this mission of the Triune God to the world involves
'God's turning to the world in respect of creation, care, redemption
and consummation' (Bosch, 1991, p. 391). It is therefore a mission
that includes proclaiming the good news of the Kingdom; teaching,
nurturing and baptizing new believers; responding to human need

by loving service; transforming unjust structures in society and safe-guarding the integrity of creation (see also the 'Marks of Mission' as devised by the House of Bishops). If mission embraces these great aims in the power of the Spirit the question remains: how best is this to be done in the context of the modern world and the paradigm shifts that have occurred and in the context of the place of the church in British society today?

A great deal of thought has gone into answering this question, in both the institutional churches as well as in new and ethnic churches in Britain today. Speaking from within one of the institutional churches (by which I mean churches with histories that go back to the early twentieth century and beyond), the most important landmark in thought on this question from within my own institutional church as well as Methodism, which has both reflected and urged missional change, was the report *Mission-shaped Church* (Church House Publishing, 2004). Many of the principles of mission already written of in this chapter are to be found there. But what the report and the movement that it reflects have done is to open up various possibilities of 'being' or 'doing' church missionally today. Archbishop Rowan Williams' phrase of a 'mixed economy' church admirably sums up the variety of so-called traditional church and 'Fresh Expressions' of church which have arisen within the Church of England today. And, more broadly, what we have in all institutional churches, as well as in many ethnic and newer churches too, is a pattern of 'being church' which is dependent on ordained ministry, permanent or semi-permanent (e.g. hired) buildings, and a structure of denominational support of varying degrees. Part of Frost's argument in his book *Exiles* is that

> I am not suggesting that there is anything inherently wrong with seminaries, denominations, church buildings, and the rest of the massive infrastructure that the church in the West has at its disposal. What I'm saying is that our reliance on them is limiting our spiritual growth. We are not fully realizing our calling to be the church of Jesus Christ as long as we rely on money, buildings, and paid experts.
>
> (Frost, 2006, p. 139)

In the well-known story of a foreigner asking directions to Dublin of an Irishman, he laconically replies, 'Oh to be sure, if I were going to Dublin, I wouldn't be starting from here!' The place from which we start mission today in Britain (with the blessings and the burdens of 1,700 years of church history since the arrival of Christianity in Britain with the Romans) may not be what we would have chosen, but there is no alternative. That being so we have three options:

1 either carrying on regardless of all that has happened in the past sixty years of social and spiritual upheaval, as undoubtedly some congregations do;
2 cutting loose from the quaint old institutions and begining something entirely new like Frosts 'smallboatbigsea' community (see <www.smallboatbigsea.org>) which meets on the outskirts of Sydney and has abandoned long sermons, long singing and long liturgy for much more interactive listening to God and each other discerning and affirming God's mission through each of its members;
3 beginning new missional communities, giving permission for their existence literally *alongside* the older traditional model of church which itself needs to renew its mission along the lines indicated in this chapter.

In the Church of England we are moving forward along the 'mixed economy' of the third option. However, it is vital to stress that the principles of mission outlined in this chapter for the church facing exile today are not optional, but essential in responding to the position we find ourselves in in this post-Christian society, whether the model for church is a 'fresh expression' or of a more traditional kind. And both models need to be supported by excellence in teaching, fellowship, pastoral care, worship and prayer. These are the elements of 'deep church' without whose continual deepening it would never become what it was intended to be (see Stott, 2007).

In the New Testament there are two models of church presented to us in the early chapters of Acts. They are the church in Jerusalem and the church in Antioch. They are often contrasted, in a slightly caricatured way, with Jerusalem being 'old church' and Antioch as being 'a fresh expression or more missional church'. The contrast is not entirely true, for nothing was more radical or possibly more powerful than the life of the church in Jerusalem, certainly at first, as depicted by Luke in this description:

> All the believers were one in heart and mind. No-one claimed that
> any of his possessions was his own, but they shared everything they

had. With great power the apostles continued to testify to the resurrection of the Lord Jesus, and much grace was upon them all.

(Acts 4.32, 33)

But the comparison is partly right in that its surmise that the second generation of Christians in Jerusalem around AD 55–60 were no longer distinguished by discernible missional activity. Maybe they were overwhelmed by the famines that came to Judea, about which Agabus prophesied, and which Paul tried to relieve through his collection among the Gentile churches (Acts 11.28), or maybe the political conditions before the Jewish Rebellion against the Romans in AD 66 drained their resources. But unlike Antioch, which remained a base for Gentile mission well into the second century, Jerusalem appeared to settle for being a centre for orthodoxy but with little missionary fire.

> The Antioch church by any standards was a remarkable body of people . . . In Antioch it soon became clear that the community was neither Jewish nor 'traditionally' Gentile, but constituted a third entity. Luke mentions that it was here that the disciples were first called 'Christians' (Acts 11.26). (See Bosch, 1991, p. 43)

The lesson is that unless we are willing to adapt the shape of our mission without diminishing the content of the gospel, then we will be not only exiles from a world that has moved on, but a museum which few will visit.

Whether it is through an intentional fresh expression of church or through the renewal of a traditional expression of church, the church in Britain needs to be constantly challenged along the principles we have considered in this chapter. Is it incarnational, making real the life of Jesus in loving service to its own community? Is its mission contextual, properly related to the community in which it is set? Is it spiritual, truly developing the spiritual journey of its members in a way that is attractive and real to outsiders too? Is it communal, witnessing to the unity and diversity in a context of truth and love? Is it relational, in which relationships flourish and are enriched by belonging to this community, enjoying table fellowship of the richest kinds together? And lastly is it missional, evidently there for the world and not itself? Such a church is well placed to live as exiles missionally with confidence and hope.

8

Singing the Lord's song in a strange land

For the church, especially the institutional churches, 'the land' has indeed changed; it is at once both familiar and unfamiliar. The countryside and towns are dotted with the spires and towers of Christendom, literally every few miles; but the context in which they bear witness to the faith of their ancestors has profoundly changed. The culture is consumerist rather than Christian, the government committed to ensuring fair play among the competing claims of religious minorities of which Christianity is one, numbering, in terms of church attendance, only about 3 per cent more than the Muslim community in Britain. The controversy in early 2008 over Archbishop Rowan Williams' foray into the place of Sharia law in Britain may only serve in retrospect to strengthen the idea that the secular state is best placed to ensure that all religions are held in plurality without favouring any one of them. The question he raised as to what extent religious scruples of different faith communities might be recognized by the law is an evolving one, but there was an emphatic answer from the nation that all should be rightly subject to laws enacted in Westminster. That has both strengths and dangers, particularly as the state becomes more secular. So, for the time being, only very limited areas of self-governance, such as disputes in marriage, are capable of voluntary resolution, for instance in Jewish religious courts. However, the resolutions of these 'courts' are voluntary and appeal to the civil courts is still a legal right.

Although much of our law is certainly profoundly based on Judeo-Christian principles, it faces complex questions which arise from scientific progress. The advance of science and in particular science to do with genetics and reproduction poses deep challenges to this Judeo-Christian ethic, not least in the context of parenthood (for example, in the right to have all biological parents stated on birth certificates where assisted conception by donor is the case), and in the context of research on hybrid embryos; and in these areas the secular state is more likely to respond in a utilitarian than an absolutist way. And although euthanasia has been recently debated and ruled out by Parliament, it may well return as an issue seeking legislative support in the future. Although Christians may be a minority in society, they still have a duty to hold leaders and legislators to account by appealing to their consciences in the decisions they take.

In these and many other ways the land, while still familiar, has changed greatly in the past forty years, and is likely to continue to do so. The church finds itself in a greater sense of exile in Britain than any time in the past 1,500 years. It has entered a new paradigm, and it has new opportunities to which it must respond not with a shrug of the shoulders, or with a strong dose of nostalgia, but with renewed compassion and commitment to the society in which we dwell, however strange and difficult it has become. After all, it is for society or the world that God gave his only Son. Often we are tempted to think that God gave his Son for the church, when in fact it was for the world (John 3.16). So how might it be possible for the church in Britain to sing the Lord's song in a foreign land? Or to put it in non-metaphorical language, how might the church flourish in exile and pursue faithfully and confidently its vocation in the world?

First, there must be an acceptance that the land *is* foreign or, to put it the other way round, that the world constructed by humankind is alien to God's Kingdom, despite the years of Christendom that have preceded and which to a certain extent still hide the full extent of the change. Of course, we may be able to point to the legacies that remain in our culture, constitution and law, some of which are referred to as 'British values' such as tolerance, equality before the law, freedom to worship, and care for the vulnerable, to name but a few. But if the historical process identified in the central section of the book still has some way to run (although arguably it could be overturned by an extraordinary Christian revival), which I believe it has, before the present paradigm is overtaken by another, the process of secularization may well continue apace. Part of accepting that the land is *foreign* though *familiar* is not simply to hark back (for those who are old enough, i.e. the over-50s, and for them this poses the greatest challenge) to the good old days before this exile took root, when 40 per cent of children went to Sunday School, when there were apparently absolute moral standards, when families stuck together, when pluralism was not a term even known, let alone experienced, when vast crowds gathered to listen to a well-known evangelist – good as these things were. It is to agree that the world has changed and that the church and the conduct of its mission must change too. It also needs to be recognized that the mission of the church in the past was sometimes a mixture of the noble and the painfully blinkered, often tied up in attitudes of prejudice towards the predicament and position of others. For example, the Magdalene Asylums for fallen women (so shockingly depicted in the 2002 film *The Magdalene Sisters*) show the extent to which mission can be infiltrated by prejudice and lack of compassion. That type of Britain has gone and it is probably set to change yet further. So we must go further back, not in our own memories but in our collective biblical memory, to stories of great risk and excitement, *dangerous stories,* (see Frost, 2006, p. 11), to whose principles we are once again called.

When the exiles sat down and wept in Babylon, they literally did not think how, on that bit of earth, they could sing the Lord's song in a foreign land, with their captors all around. But over time they learnt to. They learnt to serve the empire where they had been placed, and to do so with great courage and integrity, with some notable examples. They dug deep into their own faith stories from the past to give courage, freedom and hope in their following of God where they were. Their horizons were extended painfully from narrowly religious ones to ones that embraced the world. It was also the place to imagine, in prayerful reflection stimulated by the prophetic word, a different type of future. We shall finally trace these four *musical phrases* (as we might call them) in the Lord's song to be sung in this familiar but foreign land today.

Digging deep

When the exiles who arrived in Babylon were taunted by their captors to sing one of the songs of Zion in this strange land, where next to nothing was familiar, they must have wondered how on *that* piece of earth they could ever sing one of the Lord's songs again. As we have considered before, they must have racked their souls to discover how all the promises that God had given them could have ended up here in their captivity and despair, and how their own land which was so fertile had become a desert to them (Jeremiah 9.10–14). To rediscover their sense of purpose and vocation they had to dig deep into their Scriptures as well as create new stories of God's faithfulness and power for them while in the midst of exile. The stories which must have meant most were of their *origins* as the people of God; the call of Abraham to leave his settled existence and to go to a place that God would show him, to begin his wanderings expectant that God would guide him in the way that he should go; the provision of God for his people in the desert in an earlier Exodus when there was nothing to commend it except the dependence on God it enforced; and the more recent messages of their Prophets, not least Jeremiah, who bemoaned the corruption of their spiritual life, the desecration of the land resulting from moral failure (see Northcott, 2007, p. 5) and the endless idolatry to which they had succumbed (see the plaintive cry of Jeremiah 2.13ff). These were *dangerous stories* which would unsettle and disturb and remind the people of a way of life and pilgrimage which they had abandoned and yet to which they were once again called.

And then there was the rich contemporary witness that was around them in their captivity: the powerful prophecy of Ezekiel who accompanied them and who prophesied judgement and hope, the extraordinary prophecies of Second Isaiah (to which we shall return) as well as the new dangerous stories of Daniel and Esther. Daniel provided a new model of both resistance and compliance for the exiles: on the one hand he was willing to work for the host empire (see 6.3), but he was unwilling to compromise his fierce loyalty to the God of his fathers. Unwilling to eat the choice food of the Empire (Daniel 1.8ff) and unwilling to pray to another God, so risking death in the lions' den (6.6ff). Here was a new Joseph, at the heart of the empire but untainted by it. Likewise Esther provided a *dangerous story* for the people in captivity to cherish and be nourished by. Warned by Mordecai of the impending holocaust of the Jews in Persia, he memorably says to her as the Emperor's Queen, 'And who knows but that you have come to royal position for such a time as this?' (Esther 4.14b). Her courage and faith foils Haman's plot and the story of deliverance stands as a new rallying point for the people facing exile then and in the future.

It was from these accounts of people who sang the Lord's song in a foreign land that the Jewish nation took courage so that they too could sing again. And likewise Christians draw strength not only from these stories but more profoundly still from the double descent of the Son of God, the most *dangerous story* of them all. The *double descent*, which was gloriously reversed, was first, the descent to incarnation and, second, the descent to death on a cross or crucifixion to become *the* exile who gives life and courage. In so doing Jesus has marked out a route for us which, although not redemptive in the sense that his once-for-all-sacrifice was, is nevertheless a dynamic path for the church to follow in its own kind of exile. For, as Jesus himself said, 'Unless a grain of wheat falls to the ground and dies, it remains only a single seed. But if it dies, it produces many seeds' (John 12.23). Jesus gave up rank, privileges and status as being things incapable of being grasped or even incorporated into his incarnational life, leading to the humiliation and glory of the cross – and so should the church. It is this route marked out by *the great exile* that provides the key for singing the Lord's song in a foreign land.

So digging deep into these stories was the way the Jews in Babylon and Christians in our own Babylon will find strength and courage, reassurance and inspiration to sing the Lord's song now. And they will do so while, like Daniel, they are able to be both compliant and resistant to the demands of our host empire (see Frost, 2006, ch. 8).

Faithfully serving the host empire

The empires of this world belong to the evil one. This is made plain by the temptations of Jesus in which the devil, from the top of a high mountain offers Jesus all the kingdoms of the world if he would bow down and worship him. It was never a temptation that Jesus would accept (although it was a real one, i.e. a choice) but it implies that it was the devil's to offer. In some way the empires of the world, the power structures created by people, are all in need of redemption. To prevent their putrefaction Christians like salt should serve faithfully in them, upholding all that is good about them and keeping at bay all that it is damaging and corrupting. Exile does not mean withdrawal unless it is a withdrawal, as in the case of monks, to pray for the world and its institutions which they have left, else the withdrawal would become selfish. Working for the host empires in all their many bodies will provide ample scope both for the fulfilment of our individual gifting as well as opportunities to shape for good the way that bit of the empire works, whether it is in science, education, business, government or in some other sphere; and in so working we reflect the creative and providential side of God's grace. After all, God sustains the universe with the word of his power. He constantly provides for and is involved with his creation, so in teaching, doing business or art, medicine, creating useful software or sweeping the streets we are each involved in creatively working for the host empires, and though in exile we are nonetheless fulfilling our own gifts and taking forward God's care and provision for his creation. We can then sing the Lord's song when we do those things, humming the tune – metaphorically speaking, else we will annoy our neighbours while we work! But if on the one hand we can wholeheartedly join in, serving the host empire, there are boundaries or limits to our involvement. If our involvement harmfully affects the planet or infringes another's legitimate human rights or perpetuates or even promotes injustice then we have crossed a boundary whereby our involvement with the host empire becomes oppressive and not sustaining. Then it is time to quit, to face the lions like Daniel, to blow the whistle at work rather than to joyfully hum. The boundary set down by Micah has been crossed (see Micah 6.8) and we cannot sing the Lord's song unless we challenge the precepts of the empire.

Holding together: creating a single horizon

For centuries and still today the bane of the church's life has been dualism in which Christians separate what God has put together. In place of several horizons, or often two, Christians need a single horizon. Exile may well be the place where they learn it, as old horizons are set aside by a renewed vision of God and his greatness and we learn to sing the Lord's song under the refining influence of 'the foreign land'.

A long time ago a basic dualism was assumed by the Manichees, who held that good and evil are equal and opposite forces which involve us in a cosmic struggle in which the outcome is uncertain. The resurrection has put paid to all that; a final victorious outcome for God's Kingdom and his Christ is now assured through the raising up of Jesus by the Father. And Augustine, who had played with Manichaeism before his conversion in the garden in Milan, came to understand this. In the medieval world the dualism was distinctly between the church and the rest of the world outside it; the church provided safety, salvation and care in return for obedience; everything outside was damned. It was plain and simple. But when the church itself became corrupt, the premise for this dualism was removed. After the Enlightenment the dualism was between the sacred and the secular; the secular was underpinned by science and reason while the sacred was preserved by faith. When the worlds of faith and reason collided as they did with Galileo and Darwin either the boundaries were redrawn or faith denied the possibility of what reason suggested. The problem was that each sphere claimed what was not rightfully theirs, science turning itself into faith or faith turning itself into a scientific programme. Other dualisms exist within the church, like the separation of word from spirit, or theology from spirituality (see Smail, 2007, p. 8, where he makes a plea for the best of Karl Bath and Thomas Merton), the ordinary from the extraordinary (see Frost, 2000) and the doctrine of creation from redemption. As is so often the case with God, who is over all, above all and in all, and who sustains everything by the Word of his power (see Colossians 1.15–17) it is not a question of either/or but both/and. He is the God of word and spirit, the ordinary and the extraordinary, of reason and promise (the God-end of faith), of church and world (for he works in both always) and of good and evil (for, as Luther said, the evil one is God's devil).

Now the Israelites before the exile had fallen into all kinds of dualism. They had separated liturgy from ethics, until God told them he despised their songs, fasts and solemn assemblies. They separated worship from holiness and true vision, so that the Temple, the end of their religious horizons, had to be demolished. His promise to them had not led to obedient faith but to complacent superiority and an abandonment of their mission to be a light to the gentiles. Exile helped to end their dualisms, to recognize that God was the God of all nations, his redemption was for all people, his concern was for all their life, not just the 'religious bits', and his purpose was universal. Nowhere was this more majestically stated than in Second Isaiah (40—55). So if the church in Britain is in a new kind of exile then it is time to root out all dualisms, to regain a single horizon, to hold together what God has joined and to stop divorcing aspects of our lives from each other, which God hates. Regaining this true perspective is like assembling an orchestra and massed choir to sing the Lord's song, as when Daniel Barenboim played the 'Berliner Luft' to the people of East Germany in the open air after the fall of the Berlin Wall. They were liberated to truly understand their identity and vocation. Likewise the exiles came to understand their identity and vocation through the prophetic voice that spoke to them in exile.

An assured future

What became certain through the prophetic word, particularly through the latter chapters of Isaiah (40—66) and through the prophecies of hope in Ezekiel, was that this exile was *temporary*. Likewise all Christians know that their exile on earth is temporary. The songs we sing are in large part the anticipation of the end of exile, a rejoicing-in now of what will be fully be known and for all to see then, namely the fulfilment of God's Kingdom and the Kingdom of his Christ. The Servant Christ was prophesied in Isaiah while the exiles considered their future in Babylon. In Isaiah 52 the future is joyfully predicted. The people will leave exile. They will

> Burst into songs of joy together,
>   you ruins of Jerusalem,
> for the LORD has comforted his people,
>   he has redeemed Jerusalem.
> The LORD will lay bare his holy arm
>   in the sight of all the nations,
> and all the ends of the earth will see
>   the salvation of our God . . .
> You will not leave in haste
>   or go in flight;
> for the LORD will go before you,
>   the God of Israel will be your rearguard.
>   (Isaiah 52.9–10, 12)

In other words their future was assured, however difficult it was for a time. Jeremiah and Ezekiel had prophesied the same. Jeremiah in his letter to the exiles spoke 'of a future and an hope', and later of a new Covenant (Jeremiah 33) and Ezekiel spoke too of a new Covenant and of a revived people (see Ezekiel 36.24ff and 37.1–14). Exile was for a time. God would not abandon his people or his purposes. Confident of this knowledge, they could eventually sing the Lord's song in a foreign land until finally they would 'burst into songs of joy together'.

For the church in Britain, we face not only that common exile of all Christian people in all ages, waiting for the fulfilment of the Kingdom of God and the reality of heaven, but more particularly a kind of exile which the church in these islands has not experienced for 15 hundred years. We have endeavoured to see why that is and what accounts for this new post-Christian and end-of-Christendom experience which is widely acknowledged. Some may say that we are not in a foreign land; others may say it has only been briefly submerged. But if the historical process is right (it can of course be sovereignly reversed by God), then we are at the early stages of a new paradigm which most probably has further to develop; and the old order set up by centuries of Christendom probably has further to unravel. At the same time new challenges to the planet about sharing the earth's resources more equitably are ever more critically before us. It is in this context that the church is in a kind of exile, and more especially the institutional church which accounts for about two thirds of Christians in Britain. The other churches based on ethnicity, or greater appeal to our culture, or fresh ways of being church, are in a more flexible position to respond to the changing paradigm, although they too share in the common Christian sense of exile. Institutional church is gradually and painfully learning to respond with flexibility, but ever so slowly as it seeks both to uphold the institution and respond to the new paradigm. There is a call to new ways of conducting mission, set in new missional communities whether with an old or a new shell, with a spirituality and attitude which is both nurturing and appealing to those outside and inside. Indeed the realistic way to understand our position today is as exiles; and exile need not be feared. There are more than enough examples of its dynamic both in the Scriptures and, as we have seen, in church history to help us both to live in the experience and to make it a reforming friend rather than a fearsome judge. We have charted the course of many exiles in the first and second millennia: some wrestled with an antagonistic culture, others with opposition from within the church and others with God-denying forces in the political establishment and empires they inhabited. It is time to be inspired by the exile they suffered or embraced and nerve ourselves for the present predicament of the church in Britain. Exile was the cost of change both in Israel's history and in the succeeding paradigms of church history. Exile refines, re-forms and renews both our own vision of God as well as his call on our lives. It is time to recognize the kind of exile we are in; embrace and learn from it, knowing that through the solitary and costly life and death of *one exile* our salvation came. So we need to prepare for exile with hope, confidence and conviction; singing the Lord's song in this familiar but now strange land.

Bibliography

The dates given here refer to the edition or reprint consulted.

Alexander, Sidney (1978), *Marc Chagall: A Biography*. G. P. Putnam's Sons.

Ashworth, Jacinta and Farthing, Ian (2007), *Churchgoing in the UK: A Research Report from Tearfund on Church Attendance in the UK*. Tearfund.

Atkinson, David J., Field, David F., Holmes, Arthur and O'Donovan, Oliver, eds (1995), *New Dictionary of Christian Ethics and Pastoral Theology*. Inter-Varsity Press.

Atkinson, James (1965), *Martin Luther and the Birth of Protestantism*. Pelican.

Barker, Juliet (2005), *Agincourt: The King, the Campaign, the Battle*. Little, Brown.

Barth, Karl (1972), *Epistle to the Romans*. Oxford University Press.

Bartley, Jonathan (2006), *Faith and Politics after Christendom*. Paternoster.

Bede, The Venerable, tr. Leo Shirley-Price (1955), *A History of the English Church and People*. Penguin.

Beeson, Trevor (1974), *Discretion and Valour: Religious Conditions in Russia and Eastern Europe*. Collins.

Benedict, tr. Timothy Fry OSB (1982), *The Rule of St Benedict*. The Liturgical Press.

Black, Conrad (2004), *Franklin Delano Roosevelt: Champion of Freedom*. Phoenix.

Bosch, David J. (1991), *Transforming Mission: Paradigm Shifts in Theology of Mission*. Orbis Books.

Brierley, Peter (2006), *Pulling Out of the Nosedive: A Contemporary Picture of Churchgoing*. Christian Research.

Brown, Callum G. (2001), *The Death of Christian Britain*. Routledge.

Brueggemann, Walter (1997), *Cadences of Home: Preaching among Exiles*. Westminster John Knox Press.

Brueggemann, Walter (2001), *The Prophetic Imagination*. Augsburg Fortress.

Brueggemann, Walter (2002), *An Introduction to the Old Testament: The Canon and Christian Imagination*. Westminster John Knox Press.

Chadwick, Henry (1993), *The Early Church*. Penguin.

Chadwick, Henry (2001), *Augustine: A Very Short Introduction*. Oxford University Press.

Chadwick, Owen (1973), *The Reformation*. Penguin.

Chadwick, Owen (1990), *Michael Ramsey: A Life*. Oxford University Press.

Chadwick, Owen (1992), *The Christian Church in the Cold War*. Penguin.

Chrysostom, John, *see* Roberts, Alexander and Donaldson, James (1975).

Church of England Mission and Public Affairs Council (2004), *Mission-shaped Church: Church Planting and Fresh Expressions of Church in a Changing Context*. Church House Publishing.

Connor, James A. (2006), *Pascal's Wager: The Man Who Played Dice with God*. Harper San Francisco.

Cragg, Gerald (1972), *The Church and the Age of Reason 1648–1789*. Penguin.

Croft, Steven (2002), *Transforming Communities*. Darton, Longman & Todd.

Croft, Steven (2007), 'A Mission-Shaped Church Is Not Enough: Address to Portsmouth Diocesan Conference'.

de Waal, Esther (1999), *Seeking God: The Way of St Benedict*. Canterbury Press.

Donovan, Vincent J. (2005), *Christianity Rediscovered*. Orbis Books.

Doyle, William (2001), *The French Revolution: A Very Short Introduction*. Oxford University Press.

Dragas, George Dion (2005), *Saint Athanasius of Alexandria: Original Research and New Perspectives*. Orthodox Research Institute.

Drane, John (2006), *The McDonaldization of the Church*. Darton, Longman & Todd.

du Boulay, Shirley (1991), *Teresa of Avila*. Hodder & Stoughton.

Epistle to Diognetus, *see* Roberts, Alexander and Donaldson, James (1975).

Feiling, Keith (1963), *A History of England*. Macmillan.

Ferguson, Niall (2004), *Empire: How Britain Made the Modern World*. Penguin.

Figes, Orlando (2001), *Natasha's Dance*. Penguin.

Flower OCD, Marjorie (2002), *Centred on Love: The Poems of St John of the Cross*. Carmelite Nuns of Varroville.

Frost, Michael (2000), *Seeing God in the Ordinary: A Theology of the Everyday*. Hendrickson.

Frost, Michael (2006), *Exiles: Living Intentionally in a Post-Christian Culture*. Hendrickson.

Frost, Michael and Hirsch, Alan (2007), *The Shaping of Things to Come: Innovation and Mission for the 21st Century*. Hendrickson.

Galli, Mark (2002), *Francis Assisi and His World*. Lion.

Gilbert, Martin (2000), *The Second World War*. Phoenix.

Glenny, Misha (2000), *The Balkans*. Granta Books.

Grant, Robert M. (1997), *Irenaeus of Lyons*. Routledge.

Grigg, John (1997), *Lloyd George, The People's Champion 1902–1911*. Penguin.

Hastings, Adrian (1986), *A History of English Christianity*. Collins.

Holdsworth, John (2003), *Dwelling in Strange Land*. Canterbury Press.

Horne, Alistair (1989), *Macmillan Vol II: 1957–1986*. Macmillan.

Jenkins, Philip (2002), *The Next Christendom: The Coming of Global Christianity*. Oxford University Press.

Jenkins, Roy (1991), *A Life at the Centre*. Macmillan.

Kelly, J. N. D. (1960), *Early Christian Doctrines*. Adam & Charles Black.

Küng, Hans (1995), *Christianity: Its Essence/The Religious Situation of Our Time*. SCM Press.

Laird, Martin (2006), *Into the Silent Land: The Practice of Contemplation*. Darton, Longman & Todd.

Lampe, G. W. H., ed. (1959), *Cambridge History of the Bible Vol II: The West from the Fathers to the Reformation*. Cambridge University Press.

Lane Fox, Robin (1986), *Pagans and Christians*. Penguin.

Lane Fox, Robin (2005), *The Classical World: An Epic History from Homer to Hadrian*. Allen Lane.

Leech, Kenneth (2001), *Through Our Long Exile*. Darton, Longman & Todd.

Lehane, Brendan (2005), *Early Celtic Christianity*. Continuum.

Luther, Martin (1959), *Luther's Works Vol. 31*, ed. Harold J. Grim, tr. W. A. Lambert. Fortress Press.

MacCulloch, Diarmaid (2003), *Reformation: Europe's House Divided 1490–1700*. Allen Lane.

MacCulloch, Diarmaid (2007), *Thomas Cranmer: A Life*. Yale University Press.

McGrath, Alastair (1993), *The Renewal of Anglicanism*. SPCK.

MacIntyre, Alasdair (1981), *After Virtue*. Duckworth.

MacMillan, Margaret (2001), *The Peacemakers: The Paris Peace Conference of 1919 and Its Attempt to End War*. John Murray.

Matthew, Iain (1995), *The Impact of God: Soundings from St John of The Cross*. Hodder and Stoughton.

Moltmann, Jürgen (1977), *The Church in the Power of the Spirit*. HarperSanFrancisco.

Moreux, Serge (1949), 'Prokofiev: An Intimate Portrait', *Tempo*. New Series No. 11.

Morgan, Alison (2004), *The Wild Gospel: Bringing Truth to Life*. Monarch.

Morisy, Ann (2004), *Journeying Out: A New Approach to Christian Mission*. Morehouse.

Moynagh, Michael (2004), *Emergingchurch.intro*. Monarch.

Murray, Stuart (2004), *Post-Christendom: Church and Mission in a Strange New World*. Authentic Media.

Murray, Stuart (2005), *Church after Christendom*. Paternoster.

Mursell, Gordon (2005), *Praying in Exile*. Darton, Longman & Todd.

Neill, Stephen and Chadwick, Owen (1990), *A History of Christian Missions*. Penguin.

Newbigin, Lesslie (1989), *The Gospel in a Pluralist Society*. SPCK.

Nicholson, Adam (2003), *The Making of the King James Bible*. HarperCollins Perennial.

Northcott, Michael S. (2007), *A Moral Climate: The Ethics of Global Warming*. Darton, Longman & Todd.

O'Donovan, Oliver (2003), *The Desire of Nations: Rediscovering the Roots of Political Theology*. Cambridge University Press.

Packer, J. I. (1996), *Among God's Giants: Puritan Vision of the Christian Life*. Kingsway.

Parker, T. H. L. (1975), *John Calvin*. J. N. Dent & Son.

Pollock, John (1972), *Wilberforce*. Constable.

Pollock, John (1989), *John Wesley, 1703–1791*. Hodder & Stoughton.

Reid, Anna (1997), *Borderlands: A Journey through the History of the Ukraine*. Phoenix.

Roberts, Alexander and Donaldson, James, eds (1975) *The Nicene and Post-Nicene Fathers Vol. IX* (John Chrysostom). Eerdmans.

Roberts, Alexander and Donaldson, James, eds (1987), *Ante-Nicene Fathers: The Writings of the Fathers down to AD 325 Vol. I (Epistle to Diognetus)*. Eerdmans.

Roberts, Monty (1997), *The Man Who Listens to Horses*. Arrow Books.

Rolle, Richard, tr. Clifton Wolters (1972), *The Fire of Love*. Penguin.

Runciman, Steven (1990), *A History of the Crusades Vols I–III*. Penguin.

Russell, Bertrand (1927), *Why I Am Not a Christian*. Watts.

Russell, Bertrand (2004), *History of Western Philosophy*. Routledge Classics.

Schama, Simon (1989), *Citizens: A Chronicle of the French Revolution*. Viking.

Schama, Simon (1991), *The Embarrassment of Riches: An Interpretation of Dutch Culture in the Golden Age*. Fontana.

Smail, Tom (2007), *Praying with Paul*. Bible Reading Fellowship.

Southern, R. W. (1970), *Western Society and the Church in the Middle Ages*. Penguin.

Stackhouse, Ian (2004), *The Gospel-Driven Church*. Paternoster.

Stenton, F. M. (1967), *Anglo-Saxon England*. Oxford University Press.

Stevenson, David L. (2004), *1914–1918*. Penguin.

Stevenson, J. and Frend, W. H. C., eds (1975), *A New Eusebius: Documents Illustrating the History of the Church to AD 337*. SPCK.

Storkey, Elaine (1995), *The Search for Intimacy*. Hodder & Stoughton.

Stott, John (1992), *Contemporary Christian: Applying God's Word to Today's World*. Inter-Varsity Press.

Stott, John (2007), *The Living Church*. Inter-Varsity Press.

Thomson, Robert W., ed. (1971), *Athanasius, Contra Gentes and De Incarnatione*. Oxford University Press.

Tomkins, Stephen (2003), *John Wesley: A Biography*. Lion.

Tomlin, Graham (2002), *Luther and his World*. Lion.

Tomlin, Graham (2002), *The Provocative Church*. SPCK.

Vassiltchikov, Maria (1999), *The Berlin Diaries 1940–1945*. Pimlico.

Volf, Miroslav (2006), *Free of Charge: Giving and Forgiving in a Culture Stripped of Grace*. Zondervan.

Ware, Timothy (1997), *The Orthodox Church*. Penguin.

Whitworth, Patrick (2003), *Becoming Fully Human*. Terra Nova.
Whitworth, Patrick (2006), *Becoming a Citizen of the Kingdom*. Terra Nova.
Whitworth, R. H. (2006), *Field Marshall Lord Ligonier*. Ken Trotman.
Wright, N. T. (1992), *The New Testament and the People of God*. SPCK.
Wright, N. T. (1996), *Jesus and the Victory of God*. SPCK.
Wroe, Martin and Doney, Malcolm (2004), *The Rough Guide to a Better World*. Rough Guides/DfID.
Zeldin, Theodore (1995), *An Intimate History of Humanity*. Minerva.

Index

Index

Broughton Hall, Northamptonshire xviii
Brown, Callum 33
Brown, Gordon 30
Brueggemann, Walter 3, 9, 105–6
  Preaching to Exiles 120
Brunner, Emil 111
Bunyan, John
  The Pilgrim's Progress 103

Callistus, Bishop 39
Calvinism 54
Carmelite order 84
Carthage 40–1
Cassian, John 67
  Institutes 67
Chadwick, H. 39, 42, 61, 65, 83
Chadwick, Owen 88
Chagall, Marc xvi–xvii
Charlemagne, king of the Franks 46, 48,
  71
Charles V, Holy Roman Emperor 54, 55
Charles I, king of England 54
Charles Martel 71
Chilton, Charles
  Oh! What a Lovely War 19–20
Christendom xi–xii, 19, 123
  birth of 41, 45
  end of 29–33, 36, 96
Christian mysticism 84
Christian organizations 114
Christian Unions 32
Christianity
  Celtic 68–72, 92
  spread of 38–9
  unique claims of 23
Christianity Rediscovered (Donovan)
  116–17
*Christianity: The Religious Situation of
  Our Time* (Küng) 37, 45, 46, 49, 54,
  56, 75, 81, 84
Christina, Queen of Sweden 57
Christmas 96–7
Chronicles, Bible books of 4
church
  institutional 34, 35, 96, 122, 125, 129,
    133, 141
  membership 33–6, 96–7
  mission-focused 128–31
  models of 130–1
  patronage system 30

persecution of in Apostolic era 37–41
  see also church history
Church after Christendom (Murray) 29
church history
  early Christian apocalyptic paradigm
    37–41
  the Enlightenment 55–8, 92, 112
  Hellenistic/Greek paradigm 41–5
  Middle Ages 49–52
  the Reformation 52–5, 81, 82, 91
  Roman Catholic paradigm 45–52
Church of England 34, 115
Cistercian order 51
Clement of Alexandria 40, 42
cold war, the 20
Colman, bishop of Lindisfarne 70
Columba 69
Columbus, Christopher 55
community 124–6
  'smallboatbigsea' 130
Connor, James A. 87
conscientious objection 31–2
Constans, Roman emperor 61
Constantine, Roman emperor 29, 41, 42,
  61
Constantinople 44, 53
Constantius II, Roman emperor 61–3
Copernicus, Nicolaus 56
Councils
  Chalcedon 44
  Constance 52, 78
  Ephesus 44
  Florence 53
  Nicaea 42–3, 61
  see also Easter, dating of; Nicene Creed
Counter-Reformation 55
Cox, Harvey 25
Croft, Steven 98–9, 126
Cromwell, Oliver 54
Cromwell, Thomas 79
Crusades 50
  Fourth Crusade 74
culture, changes in 25–9, 36
Cuthbert 70, 71
Cyprian, Bishop 40–1
Cyril of Alexandria 44
Cyrus 6

Damascus 47
Daniel xiv, 10, 12, 136

150

Index